Beyond Transformative Learning in African-American Adult Education

By exploring how the religious beliefs, scientific knowledge, and social surroundings of African-American sufferers of type 2 diabetes mellitus (T2DM) impacts their understanding of the condition, this book develops a new model of effective adult learning.

Presenting the findings of rigorous qualitative research undertaken with five individuals with T2DM, this volume considers how individuals' educational background, their personal experiences, and their relationship with African-American theism have impacted on their efforts to understand and manage the disease. Identification of the social and spiritual dynamics which govern adults' acceptance of a chronic condition such as diabetes, and their ability to manage the illness according to modern medical principles, informs the development of a new theory of adult learning known as permeated learning. This model, which extends beyond transformative learning to recognize the influence of social constructs specific to African-American communities, will have broad application to adult education and the management of chronic diseases.

This scholarly text will be of great interest to graduate and postgraduate students, researchers, academics, and policymakers in the field of adult education, African-American education, transformative learning, lifelong learning, and multicultural education.

Gerald D. Redwine is Associate Professor of Clinical Laboratory Science at Texas State University, USA.

Routledge Research in Lifelong Learning and Adult Education Series

Books in this series:

Enhancing the Wellbeing and Wisdom of Older Learners
A Co-research Paradigm
Tess Maginess

Global Networks, Local Actions
Rethinking adult education policy in the 21st century
Marcella Milana

UNESCO's Utopia of Lifelong Learning
An Intellectual History
Maren Elfert

Adult Education and the Formation of Citizens
A Critical Interrogation
Andreas Fejes, Magnus Dahlstedt, and Maria Olson

How Non-Permanent Workers Learn and Develop
Challenges and Opportunities
Helen Bound, Karen Evans, Sahara Sadik and Annie Karmel

Further Education, Professional and Occupational Pedagogy
Knowledge and Experiences
Sai Loo

Beyond Transformative Learning in African-American Adult Education
Religion, Health, and Permeated Learning as a New Model of Adult Learning
Gerald D. Redwine

For more information about this series, please visit: www.routledge.com/education/series/RRLLAE

Beyond Transformative Learning in African-American Adult Education

Religion, Health, and Permeated Learning as a New Model of Adult Learning

Gerald D. Redwine

NEW YORK AND LONDON

First published 2020
by Routledge
52 Vanderbilt Avenue, New York, NY 10017

and by Routledge
2 Park Square, Milton Park, Abingdon, Oxon, OX14 4RN

Routledge is an imprint of the Taylor & Francis Group, an informa business

© 2020 Taylor & Francis

The right of Gerald D. Redwine to be identified as author of this work has been asserted by him in accordance with sections 77 and 78 of the Copyright, Designs and Patents Act 1988.

All rights reserved. No part of this book may be reprinted or reproduced or utilize in any form or by any electronic, mechanical, or other means, now known or hereafter invented, including photocopying and recording, or in any information storage or retrieval system, without permission in writing from the publishers.

Trademark notice: Product or corporate names may be trademarks or registered trademarks, and are used only for identification and explanation without intent to infringe.

Library of Congress Cataloging-in-Publication Data
A catalog record for this title has been requested

ISBN: 978-0-367-34538-9 (hbk)
ISBN: 978-0-429-32647-9 (ebk)

Typeset in Sabon
by codeMantra

To African-American living with type 2 diabetes and memorable quotes and epiphanies.

"We are digging our grave, one fork at a time, and that's what he did."

"When one has the cognition, and the ability, yet continues that habit until death, that individual is an addict."

"most of the responsibilities belong to the one who has diabetes, and their faith should be such that it is <u>active</u>, <u>advisable</u>, <u>teachable</u>, <u>practical</u>, and <u>searches</u> for answers."

"Surprised …the participants countered with vehement expressions indicating that faith and diabetes did not have any relationship. In fact, the suggestion seemed repugnant and astonishing to them."

"Faith… responding with knowledge based on their beliefs about diabetes and relying on God for circumstances beyond their control."

"growth in faith experienced by Carlos… is equivalent to self-efficacy."

"Faith is one thing, but man, don't be stupid."

Contents

List of Figures ix
List of Tables xi
Acknowledgments xiii

Introduction 1

PART 1
Laying the Foundation 3

1 Mothers, the Martyr's Response, and Afro-Theism 4
2 The Participants and the Church of God in Christ (COGIC) Subculture 9
3 Afro-Theism: Subcultural Results 16
4 The COGIC Significant Subculture 24

PART 2
Research Approach 33

5 So, What Is the Problem? 34
6 Purpose and Questions 39
7 Qualitative Research: Grounded Theory 43

PART 3
Background and Methodology 49

8 Researcher's Perspective 50
9 Theoretical Framework 53

viii *Contents*

PART 4
Data Collection and Analysis 59

10 Interviews 60
11 Search for Symbols 76
12 Data Analysis 79

PART 5
Emerging Theory 85

13 Emergent Categories: Fear and Ancestral Mentors 86
14 Emergent Categories: Fix, Fatalism, Faith, Frustration, and Authoritarian Mentors 96
15 Anatomy of Substantive Living 104
16 Substantive Living 129

PART 6
The Theory: Permeated Learning Emergence 135

17 Key Finding 136
18 Permeated Learning 142
19 Permeated Learning: Implications and Recommendations 146
20 Permeated Learning: Past to Present 149
21 Gaps Bridged: Permeated Learning Theory Applied 155

References 161
Index 169

Figures

1.1	Sunday School Teacher: Amanda Alexander	5
3.1	Autographs of First Five African-Americans Attending Texas State University and the Phi Beta Sigma Fraternity President	18
3.2	H. D. Redwine; Slave Owner's Will	21
8.1	Henry: Grandfather	50
11.1	Afro-Theistic Symbolic Interactionism–Context and Process	77
12.1	Field Notes	80
12.2	MAXQDA–Coding and Memos	81
12.3	Inspiration 9–Memos and Early Diagrams	83
13.1	FEAR–The Catalyst	87
13.2	Fear Factors	89
13.3	FEAR Affectivity	90
13.4	Afro-Theistic Change Agents	91
14.1	Dualistic Afro-Theistic Faith, Knowledge, and Social Constructs	99
15.1	Afro-Theistic Substantive Living	105
16.1	Afro-Theistic Theory in 3D	130
18.1	Permeated Learning Theory	145
20.1	Ancestors Legacy of Health	150

Tables

5.1	National Diabetes Statistics by Ethnicity	36
15.1	Code Triangulated Significance	106
15.2	Afro-Theistic Processes: Code Statistics	108

Acknowledgments

To, Gran-dear, my wife of 40 years, who made many sacrifices, including giving up countless hours to allow me time to focus on completing this body of work. For the great journey, we have shared, starting poor, but together given the grace to have careers after raising our six children. To our grandbabies Naree, Jayla, Makai, Senai, Jaliyah, Jamariyah, Jackie Lee, the fourth, and Zaza who gave us joyful breaks throughout this journey. Thank goes to the participants, of the COGIC African-American subculture and fellow lifelong learners and T2DM sufferers. Finally, thanks to the many scholars, Drs. Annie Brooks, unknowingly inspired the development of the Permeated Learning theory, Furney, Larrotta, methodology specialist, and Rohde, a scholar, and friend, to name a few that made this journey possible.

Introduction

Permeated learning, fueled by substantive living, is a theory developed from the social constructs, and spirituality of African-American with type 2 diabetes mellitus (T2DM). The purpose of this book is to explain the theory, and its development without reproducing the proof found in the dissertation (Redwine, 2015). Instead, this book emphasizes these same individuals and details of social constructivism that funneled their knowledge into the resulting model of learning. The permeated learning theory moves beyond transformative learning by delving into the learning of African-Americans with diabetes and serves in understanding how to support those in critical need of managing or abating the effects of the disease.

To begin, T2DM is the seventh leading cause of death in America, but for African-Americans, the prevalence of the disease is greater than most ethnic groups. Therefore, the urgency is to reduce the prevalence of T2DM in the African-American community through social constructs for prevention or management that is crucial for long-term survival without the debilitating effects of the disease. The immediate use of the theory is for a national campaign to reduce T2DM in the African-American community from the predicted one-in-three or 15.9% to the current (2019) 7.6% of Whites with T2DM by the year 2050. However, the beauty of the permeated learning (PL) theory, once explained, is its potential use elsewhere. That is, colleagues have seen the possible application of the theory within other cultures, with other chronic diseases, and in other life-threatening situations.

The theory developed out of an understanding that diabetes is an epidemic in the American population, but it is more prevalent among African-Americans and Mexican-Americans, with prediabetes beginning between the ages of 20 and 39. Up to this time, only a small number of qualitative research studies include the perspectives of African-American prediabetic and diabetic patients, despite being among the greatest affected per capita. Furthermore, there are gaps in the theoretical knowledge of social constructs in the diabetic community of African-American or more accurately, a conglomerate of subcultures. The failure to recognize the social influences of subcultures in African-American communities possibly contributes to the low participation in support groups that have proven to be sources of assistance in diabetes maintenance. Another gap in knowledge is how spirituality influences decisions made concerning diabetes in subcultures of African-Americans with the disease. The last exposure is a gap in understanding how faith and knowledge evolve through the social constructs of African-Americans, especially when death from diabetes is imminent.

The Church of God in Christ (COGIC) emerged as a significant African-American subculture with social constructs of adult learning, faith, and knowledge that inadvertently influence the decisions of over five million or nearly 12% of the African-Americans concerning T2DM. The COGIC is the social construct of all individuals used in the theory development where this commonality removed distracting variables. Now developed, the permeated learning theory is available for testing additional variables (groups/circumstances) beyond social constructivism of the COGIC and T2DM seen unfolding in the chapters of this book.

Part 1
Laying the Foundation

Part 1 lays the groundwork to develop a theory to help African-Americans with type 2 diabetes mellitus (T2DM) manage and prevent the disease. It serves three purposes: (i) to reveal the chronic problems of diabetes in the African-American community, (ii) to establish the influences of subcultural religious segregation, and (iii) set the background for understanding how one subculture constructs knowledge about diabetes in light of their practices of faith. Initially, the overview demonstrated the devastating effects of African-Americans attempting independent management of this insidious disease. Part 1 extracts principles of adult education relevant to the development that necessarily includes their strategies of survival through faith, knowledge, and social constructs; corroborated with Dewey (1982), in knowing how they learn; and then applied to diabetes education.

So, Chapter 1 begins with a reflective look at the effects of T2DM and adult learning. The chapter continues by giving reasons for selecting one group of African-Americans for the study. Chapter 2 continues with an introduction of the participants, and the importance of establishing rapport with them in their environment. It also introduces the choice of using the grounded theory methodology for African-Americans suffering from diabetes with a focus on faith, knowledge, and social constructs. The assessment includes a look at the adult learning theories of self-directed learning and their importance in the African-American subcultures. Chapter 3 examines the concept of Afro-Theism and subcultures. Chapter 4 concludes Part 1 with an expansion on previously discussed self-directed learning into self-efficacy, and upon reasons for selecting a social group of one church denomination, the Church of God in Christ (COGIC).

1 Mothers, the Martyr's Response, and Afro-Theism

The term Afro-Theism is developed later contextually as Black descendants of African slaves who necessarily developed a social construct around their religious belief for survival. The researcher's Afro-Theistic background serves as an example of the desperate need to understand the silent suffering of African-Americans with diabetes. Therefore, the theory developed will give the reader, educators, and qualitative researchers a new approach to understanding how chronic sufferers learn ad hoc and systematically about their affliction. In other words, the theory meets the sufferer in their daily struggles with diabetes that have invaded an already difficult life. Although the theory emerged from efforts to incorporate both the character and learning processes of one marginalized community, the findings resonate with the masses.

The research conducted in producing the permeated learning theory originated in the African-American culture, which in many ways continues to suffer from the diaspora. For these, there are daily reminders of otherness, mainly in the perceptions of non-African-Americans, some subtle and rapidly dismissed, while others are blatantly obvious and impossible to ignore. The inability to escape the color of one's skin has caused the African-American culture to become a unique and diverse ethnic group in the American society. Thanks to the civil rights movement, for some African-Americans, they are so diverse in education, jobs, positions, and all vestige of the American pursuit of happiness that the only commonality is the color of their skin. Regardless, the greater majority are those who descended from slaves, which has produced some unique influences on how these individuals in the culture learn and process the information they are privy to receiving. Historically, learning self-restraint at an early age in a hostile society was a matter of survival. Having to learn how to survive at an early age in a prejudice society was the researcher's childhood experiences in the 1960s and as a teenager in the 1970s in the South. As the emic or insider who identifies with the participants, the theory emerged from those of his and the surrounding generations who are suffering from type 2 diabetes mellitus (T2DM).

Typical of these African-Americans, education extends from the home and church and includes practical and philosophical wisdom.

Figure 1.1 Sunday school teacher: Amanda Alexander 1890–1965.

For example, imported to this study is the researcher's first philosophical discussion that came at the age of seven and still has an impact on his ontology. In 1965, at the age of seven years, Sister Amanda Alexander, his first teacher (Sunday school) outside of the home, died (see Figure 1.1). A few days before the funeral, a philosophical joust ensued because of a new word that resonated, and that word was "death." The researcher's mother had said, Sister Alexander would no longer teach the Sunday school class because she had died, and they were going to attend her funeral. The thought evoked a question,

> "What is death?" His mother's response was, "When people go to sleep and don't wake up." Why he asked. They go home to be with the Lord, she replied. After several bouts, she saw that the researcher did not understand death. She then gave him some shocking news to make her point. She said, "One day I am going to die and no longer be with you." With this revelation came the immediate understanding of death and the wailing began. In fact, he cried bitterly from that morning until two or three in the afternoon. Early on, she sent his brother to console him whom he shook off his shoulders and refused his condolence. Many years later, while serving in the Air Force, she visited him, and he asked her if she remembered the episode, to which she responded, "Yes." He said, "if you die before me know that I've already done my crying." She smiled as though she knew he would still cry, but when he did weep, it was not due to shock. He was aware that it was coming one day.

In 1991, while serving overseas, the American Red Cross informed the researcher that his mother had passed away. She was only 64 years old and had died from complications of T2DM. When the researcher received the news, he thought, "Lord it is not fair that a woman who

6 Laying the Foundation

devoted her life to answering you, her church and the community as a missionary, would die without receiving some benefit." In the 33 years of observing her, he never heard her complain or reveal personal information before, during, or after she assisted families, friends, neighbors, and church members with personal issues. In fact, she never let others know when she gave assistance or complained that those needing help were a burden. She faithfully served at her church and loved her husband, his dad, 40 years her elder, until his death at the age of 97. All family members called him Papa, whether his children, grandchildren, or in-laws, the name "Papa" was the same.

Following Papa's death, his mother went 100 percent blind within one month due to the stress surrounding the death of her husband. T2DM caused her to have periodical lapses into comas for the next six years. Despite those obstacles, she continued to serve at the country church, until living alone, blind, and complaints from family members forced her to leave what had been her home for nearly 30 years. The researcher thought he could take care of her until he realized the unreasonable expectation of his wife. He had married her when she was 18 years old, and six years later, they had four children. She had already sacrificed a career to rear their children, all under the age of eight, and adding her blind mother-in-law made that unreasonable. Due to his military obligations limiting the researcher's ability to assist his wife, and with scarce resources, with utter consternation, he sent his mother to her sister. Seeing her tears and hearing her plead to say, she would not be a burden, ripped his heart apart, but he made the best decision under the circumstances. With remorse, he thought it was so unfair that the timing was such that he could not take care of his mother, who had served everyone so well. She certainly was not deserving of continuous moves from one house to another, but diabetes was the source of this problem.

Consequently, in February 1991, while stationed at Bitburg Air Base Germany, the researcher received the dreaded call that made it impossible to make restitution to someone he owed so much. His baby brother said that one month earlier their mother surreptitiously and slowly examined his firstborn's body, and extremities, as though she was making sure her baby was a man who no longer needed her. Apparently seeing that her son had a healthy child and a wife to take care of her baby triggered a martyr's response (D. Wood, Pilisuk, & Uren, 1973), with diabetes being the executioner, since, within a month she slipped into her final coma and died. Her response seems equivalent to Watson's (2002) statement that, "The martyr is not a victim of circumstances. The martyr chooses" (p. 15). Unlike Watson's (2002) belief that "...the martyr must capture the imagination of those hearing his or her story" (p. 15), his mother would never bring attention to herself in that manner. As she would put it, "that was between her and God." Ironically, about ten years after the researcher's mother died, he also developed diabetes. After reflecting upon the circumstances of his mother's death, he panicked. He thought, "I cannot allow diabetes to kill me at an early age like it did his mother." For the next two months, he lived on soup and water and lost 40 pounds. Subsequently, doctors discontinued his prescription of Glucophage, faster than they prescribed it. With determination, he managed to keep the weight off for five years. However, over the next three years, he regained about 15 pounds, and the insidious diabetes's elevated glucose reemerged.

Furthermore, in 2011 while feverishly perplexed over the focus of his research on diabetes for a dissertation, the researcher's wife received a call stating that the ambulance had rushed her mother to a local hospital over 300 miles away. Doctors immediately started life support, all because of diabetes complications. Once the family members arrived; on the Thanksgiving Day, they decided to end life support. Consequently, the researcher, along with family members, including children, were grief-stricken as they watched her mother, affectionately known as "Grannie Reen," gasp for her last breaths of life; again diabetes. Ironically, Gran's death occurred only months after the researcher lamented to his cohorts in a History of Adult Education class that his mother-in-law's children could not see what was happening. They had taken away her privileges of independence by insisting that she eat properly, be submissive to the nurse's aide provided for her, and most of all, stop supporting a son that should be supporting her. Like with the researcher's mother, the effects of diabetes seemed to trigger a martyr's response, since, within a month, she went into a fatal coma.

In addition to the previous diabetes-related deaths, about a year before his mother-in-law's death, a first cousin in her forties died from gas gangrene. Her death was sudden and unexpected from neuropathy that caused her to be unaware of an infected toe. The emergency staff admitted her into the hospital, and the intravenous medication seemed to arrest the infection. She was conscious, in good spirits and talking one day, but the next day, she died. Also, about a year before his first cousin's death, an older brother had a kidney donated by his wife. The transplant was necessary because diabetes had destroyed his kidneys. Lastly, in 2011, doctors admitted the researcher into a local hospital while experiencing severe abdominal pain, without him realizing the cause was uncontrolled diabetes, which overwrote his belief that by faith that he was healthy.

Each of these cases of diabetes had the Church of God in Christ (COGIC) in common. The commonality of historical background, membership in, or attendance primary in a local COGIC assembly makes this an Afro-Theistic study of a subculture. From these cases and considering the prevalence of T2DM in African-Americans (CDC, 2012b) and the potential number having an association with the COGIC faith, a need was seen to focus this research on understanding this group of

African-American with diabetes. Specifically, this qualitative research sought for an Afro-Theistic theory grounded in the data of participants that explains how faith joins with diabetes education (Glesne, 2011). This discourse revealed stressors that complicates a typical African-American home, most with similarly limited resources that complicates learning and changes with chronic diseases like T2DM. The method of inquiring in developing a theory came through the interviews of the COGIC adults with diabetes. Again, the theory developed is for the benefit of those suffering from chronic diseases, especially diabetes, by providing a theory of learning for researchers and healthcare providers who work with these individuals.

2 The Participants and the Church of God in Christ (COGIC) Subculture

The selection of participants came with certain expectations based upon literature concerning commonalities of adult learners in various diseases states, primarily patients with prediabetes and type 2 diabetes mellitus (T2DM), to understand how their faith, knowledge, and social constructs worked together in managing T2DM. Identifying these diabetic patients as adult learners also classified them as self-directed learners, according to Knowles (1970). By self-directed learning, Knowles meant that these adults become lifelong learners through an inquiry about a subject, especially relevant to T2DM. Others predicted that these adult learners would typically be middle-aged self-directed learners out of necessity since managing diabetes depended upon them understanding the disease and taking necessary actions after gaining that knowledge (Kiawi et al., 2006).

The participants in this study elected to participate after an introduction to the study following a diabetes workshop sponsored by Jane (pseudonym). The five Church of God in Christ (COGIC) members with T2DM, briefly introduced below, accepted the invitation presented by Jane to the participants after a diabetes workshop. Jane was sent enough flyers for multiple participants in hopes of getting five to ten qualified. Other acquaintances were contacted to provide the additional names of potentially qualified candidates if needed for the study. Jane gave the participants instructions and the researcher's contact information to anonymously let him know that they wanted to participate. After the phone call, they received a consent form to examine, by post.

Data collection is the most crucial aspect of this study because the COGIC members with and without T2DM are private individuals who do not openly discuss private matters with strangers. Therefore, getting to know the participants is the only way to gain their trust in discussing their deepest feelings and thoughts. Since COGIC members are highly social, spending considerable time in multiple church settings, it served as an introduction to establish rapport with members of their social group, the church, as part of the interview strategy.

Interview Preparation

This study used interviews as the means of collecting data for purposive sampling of T2DM COGIC members. Conducting the interviews of COGIC members required forethought in approaching a people skeptical of outsiders. The following sections describe this process in choosing the setting and establishing rapport with the community and the participants. A digital recorder captured each interview and was downloaded directly into a password-protected computer following each session. To maintain confidentiality, each participant received a pseudonym. All data collected, including the recording, refer to the participants by their pseudonym. Most of the data consisted of an in-depth interview of the participants with semistructured open questions, but also field notes with observations.

A second factor, based on experience from the mentioned courses and with the literature review, comes in the method of data collection. The participants chose, within reason, the place of the interview as a means of ameliorating the interview interactions (Glesne, 2011). The fifth and final factor for this study is the interview guide. The experience gained in coursework, the literature review, and the theoretical framework resulted in carefully constructed interview questions that were an adaptation, by permission, from two sources. The open-ended questions only guided the conversation and used to stimulate dialog over an area the participants may have missed. However, as a guide, they proved invaluable in obtaining information on the participants' processes of combining their Afro-Theistic faith and the knowledge of T2DM through their social construct.

Weiler's (2007) interview questions for the study of the socio-culture of Latino migrant workers with T2DM served as a source for developing questions concerning diabetes knowledge and social constructs. Cordova's (2011) interview questions for the study of spirituality among T2DM patients served as a source for developing questions concerning diabetes knowledge and faith. The semistructured questions provided data from purposive sampling (Birks & Mills, 2011) of five participants. To answer the research questions in developing a theory grounded in data of how African-American COGIC diabetic adults construct meaning to reconcile their faith with the knowledge of diabetes (Glesne, 2011). These semistructured questions were flexible and allowed for the probing of other details in understanding the diabetic member's faith, knowledge of diabetes, and the Afro-Theistic constructs to interpret the data. The occasional use of additional probing questions (Merriam, 2009) helped illuminate details that clarified the participant's information.

In summary, the overarching question concerning the COGIC members' construction of knowledge, and processes involving their actions, interactions, and emotions, guided the generation of the research questions.

In turn, the research questions adapted from the two previously mentioned sources resulted in the interview questions for this study. Finally, an interview matrix (Redwine, 2015) connected the research questions to the discussion questions and suggested areas of inquiry for processes leading to a theory grounded in the participants' data.

The Setting

The participants in this study chose a meeting location that did not compromise confidentiality and where they felt relaxed with the interview. Reduced anxiety also came from the insistence on having other people nearby, whether in a house, in the church or other facilities, and with minimum disturbances. Travel distance and time were short in meeting each participant at the mutually agreed location, facilitated by modest sizes of most homes that compacted the community. The interview began with the reading of a statement to relax the participants. The statement also assured them of the importance of the study to sufferers of T2DM in the African-American community. Moreover, before the interview and the choosing of a pseudonym, the participants gave their permission to start the recording session.

The participants are in a neighborhood that included a COGIC church and many family members nearby. The church is a close-knit community of Pentecostal believers who are familiar with unique traditions that are generations old. Each community has its story of how their place of worship began. Typically, these churches will start independently of the mother church and therefore have considerable liberty in the way they conduct their services with little threat from the national organization. Each pastor expects to care for their members until death, or physically or mentally incapable. Therefore, participants with diabetes have enormous trust, especially in the pastors, followed by ordained elders and elderly church mothers. All the participants lived in the neighborhood close to the church of their fellowship.

This study took place in a COGIC community located on a coast, which began with the prayers of the migrant workers, but its organization is attributed to the efforts of one woman. Whites forced these migrant workers to live on the shores until resorts became popular. These African-Americans made the best of the situation, which was a luxury without the expenses. For example, they fished and enjoyed free fresh seafood, despite the meager living quarters. When the Whites wanted the coastal land, they forced these African-Americans to live inland by physically threatening them. As one would anticipate, someone burned the house of the last African-American on the coastal side of the railroad track, who tried to maintain what rightfully belonged to them. Once relocated, the close-knit community of relatives lived around the COGIC that most of them attended.

12   Laying the Foundation

The African-American community owes its survival to three prominent families that relocated to the area from the Deep South as migrant workers to work in the abundant citrus groves. Two of these families came from an infamous southern county while the other came from the west coast of the state. Several prominent household members in the neighborhood gained notoriety with their advancement at a U.S. government aviation facility. The notoriety started when the dad of one prominent family gained employment at the agency as a janitor and worked his way up to be an aviation jet propulsion mechanic. This job became the door of opportunity for other family members in successive generations. The children and grandchildren of this former janitor are very gifted at mathematics. However, they do not receive particular attention; in fact, one would think they were of little importance until neighbors needed a tutor when faced with problems in learning mathematics.

Rapport with the Participants' Community

The coastal community chosen resulted in a perfect microcosm of the COGIC denomination, ideal because the majority of its citizens are members of the centrally located COGIC church. Moreover, the founding of the community and church began simultaneously when migrant workers in the 1930s and 1940s came here, around the time of World War II. An elderly lady started the church and conducted services until the headquarters sent a COGIC pastor. This humble beginning typifies most COGIC churches, where inspired individuals, usually traveling preachers, started church activity, but it is not unusual for lay members to begin worship services in available facilities. Meaning, the type of building was secondary to the felt need for communal worship.

Nevertheless, this church grew into a beautiful edifice, including the rearing of celebrities. That is, the musical talent and the voice of their choir had quality enough to produce a gospel CD. Currently, one of the most talented singers is a former defensive player on a college national championship football team. He is also related to at least one of the participants in this study. The church remains humble and does not promote or publish its celebrities. Outsiders only discovered this information over time in getting to know the people of the community.

The first task in researching the COGIC subculture was to find those willing to talk about their experiences with T2DM. Participants needed to come from a community typical of COGIC churches. That is, members throughout the United States usually live in the community surrounding their COGIC church. This decision was crucial in finding participants willing to talk, especially since most in the COGIC community are suspicious of the motives of outsiders. Suspicion is also an ethnic characteristic, as discussed in Chapter 3. Fortunately, several prior visitations of the researcher to this coastal town helped establish an excellent reputation among the citizens in the community.

Additionally, having the first meetings in a previously established safe space to freely talk was important. The felt safety did not guarantee openness, but it provided the space to build trust and respect for one another. The fact is, the basis of this confidence and respect came from a mutual love for the family when introduced to the community years before. Having this rapport with the citizens are lessons learned from Vella's experiences with church authorities in Tanzania (Vella, 2002). That is, it was imperative, as a researcher, to create a safe constructivist environment where mutual learning took place. Unknowingly, this constructivist approach began long before visiting this community, not long after meeting this couple and more than 20 years before knowing this was a method of learning, let alone knowing it had a name. We spent many hours in philosophical dialogs around biblical themes and teachings. On at least one occasion, the dialog started before sunset and did not end until sunrise. This mutual respect and enjoyment of each other's philosophical knowledge and intellect quickly grew into comfort around and love for each other's family. This backdrop provided the comfort and confidence to begin this study in the community of a friend.

While wrapping up the defense of the proposal and considering how to introduce the study to this friend, an episode occurred seemingly through divine intervention. This friend's wife (also a friend), pseudonyms Jason and Jane, accidentally sent my wife an invitation to their local church event via email. Not only was Jane surprised and apologetic for the invite, knowing we were hundreds of miles away, but she was utterly shocked to hear that the research would say yes to the invite. This invitation was crucial to establishing rapport with the participants.

Establishing Rapport with the Participants

Rapport with the participants came in three phases. It began with a diabetes workshop, followed by a general introduction to the study and a packet with contact information for those interested in participating, and finally, accepting an invitation to be the guest speaker at the local COGIC church before meeting with the participants. The diabetes workshop was an unplanned addition to this study. After learning that the real purpose for visiting was diabetes research, Jane was thrilled. With seeming providence, she had started monthly health workshops at the local COGIC church because of their pastor's wife's death from T2DM. However, the workshops were nonspecific public health awareness within the community due to the death of their pastor's wife. Jane offered to focus the next workshop on T2DM as a way of providing each participant the opportunity to give feedback on a diabetes support session in addition to other experiences with T2DM.

14 *Laying the Foundation*

We worked out the details to enhance the research study without altering it. Again, with seemingly divine intervention, the nurse frequently conducting the workshops was unable to attend the meeting. As a result, Jane asked two COGIC members who had inspirational experiences with managing T2DM to facilitate the meeting. According to the attendees, these facilitators were awe-inspiring to the point that Jane regretted not video recording the entire session. Participants also revered the facilitators as mentors on how to manage their T2DM.

Jane gave general information and each attendee a packet with contact details if they wished to participate in the study of this COGIC subculture of African-Americans with T2DM. Of course, there was apprehension, due to the invasive nature of research into private lives, especially for those already skeptical about the idea. Five attendees responded immediately with others taking a wait-and-see approach. Meaning, they wanted to see if any negative feedback about the research spread throughout the community. Disguising the participants' data helped protect their identity, especially considering the town is close-knit, with citizens attending the COGIC church having genetic relationships, relationships by marriage, or long-term friendship.

Finally, having a speaking engagement at their COGIC church on Sunday before the interviews helped relax the five participants. This engagement provided an opportunity to relax the community concerning the research and included a sincerely expressed desire to help African-American suffering with T2DM. Having the participants open, forthright, and relaxed was paramount. Part of the rapport was having a shared understanding of language. For example, purposefully omitted is the term "father" from this document and replace with dad or papa. The COGIC church members avoid using the word "father" about a parent because Scripture forbids the use toward anyone other than "God the Father." Therefore, the interviews were a casual conversation of mutual understanding without regard to syntax. In other words, the language would change with outsiders.

As a result, at times, the participants did not adhere to standard sentence structures. For example, when speaking in the third person, they were giving an opinion of what they thought others likeminded COGIC members with T2DM would say. Their opinion was the first person, but they were subject to use first, second, or third person references in one sentence. However, the participants maintain control of the interview; even to the point of requesting the deletion of their data should they have changed their mind about doing the interview.

The Participants

Arianna: Arianna is in her late fifties, and she is a certified nursing assistant (CNA), which requires a high school diploma or equivalent and supervised clinical training. Arianna has been a COGIC member since childhood. Arianna was apathetic toward T2DM, convinced that she did not have the disease.

Glenn: Glenn is in his mid-fifties and a laborer that does not require education beyond high school. Glenn is a relatively new member of the COGIC denomination. Glenn is willing to fix his problems with T2DM, but he believes doctors think that he is ignorant. Because of that, he believes doctors have little interest in him.

Livia: Livia is in her early sixties and a retired registered nurse (RN), which requires a bachelor's degree or equivalent. She vacillates between believing she has T2DM and not having the disease based on what she thinks are motive driven biased test results. Livia is a COGIC member since childhood and a missionary in the church.

Carlos: Carlos is in his early fifties and for many years worked as a jet engine mechanic, which required him to have technical training at an aviation maintenance school or equivalent. He serves as a mentor for those who have T2DM. He is a COGIC elder, who is an ordained preacher with all the rights as a pastor, including pastoring a church in the denomination. Carlos is also a talented string instrumentalist.

Nick: Nick is in his mid-fifties and worked for many years as a police officer, which requires Police Academy training or equivalent. Nick serves as a mentor for those with T2DM. Nick is also a talented minister of music. Nearby, a former National Football League (NFL) player and winner of multiple NFL championships is part owner of the popular dining facility located on the coast. Several prominent members of the community are well known and liked, especially Nick, one of the participants. Nick receives hugs and kisses from the waitresses, and they know his meals, like having fish for breakfast, without him ordering, and the owners personally visit his table.

3 Afro-Theism
Subcultural Results

The following two sections review the rhetoric that coalesced into Afro-Theism with two subdivisions: Afro-Theistic faith, and Afro-Theistic constructivism as terms developed in describing African-Americans' subcultural relationship to religion which have a threefold purpose. Foremost is a deconstructed literature review that introduces the concept of Afro-Theism, followed by faith redefined as Afro-Theistic faith, and self-defined Afro-Theistic constructivism that forms the theoretical framework of the study.

Afro-Theism

The development of the theoretical framework for this study first required the establishment of terminology relevant to it. The word Afro-Theism describes today's Americans of African descent who survived the diaspora. Thus, Afro-Theism is the combination of the word Afro, which mean of African descent, and theism meaning having a belief in God. The history of African-Americans not only attest to this fact but, more importantly, explains distinct divisions within the culture. So theism both unified and divided the culture. On the one hand, religion was a sanctioned way of surviving, but denominations or nuances of beliefs or practices divided the culture.

Therefore, the African-American culture has subcultural divisions based on philosophies of church denominations or theistic viewpoints. Ironically, these subcultures are traceable to the divisions in Europe caused by the Protestant Reformation that led to the Pilgrims' flight to the Americas in the first place. However, the source of divisions within the African-American culture extends from another disagreement within the Protestant churches. This division is over the philosophies of two historical theologians, John Calvin (1509–1564) and Jacobus Arminius (1560–1609) (Enns, 1989; Ryrie, 1995). Adheres to Calvin's teaching are known as Calvinist. These are the Baptists, some Methodists, and fundamentalists in general, who maintain Martin Luther's (1483–1546) literal interpretation (hermeneutics) of biblical scriptures.

The resurgence of literal interpretation emerged as the method of choice during the Protestant Reformation (Ramm, 1970; A. S. Wood, 1995). Arminius adheres, like the Church of God in Christ (COGIC), an African-American Pentecostal denomination, and others, including some Methodists, often unknowingly adopt the Catholic concept of interpreting the biblical text through mystical or allegorized (symbolized) meanings (Ramm, 1970; A. S. Wood, 1995). Jerome, Vincent, and Augustine initiated allegorization and the idea of interpretation by church authorities, and later officially adopted and propagated by the first Roman Catholic Pope, Gregory the Great (AD 540–604), at the beginning of the Middle Ages, the predecessor of the Dark Ages (Zuck, 1991), and continues to date. Modern attraction to allegorized Scripture resulted from the development of pietism (edifying). Pietism arose from "reactions against dogmatic and fanciful" (Ramm, 1970, p. 61) post-Reformation interpretation of biblical scriptures. In short, in modernity, at the extremes, Calvinists sermons, many will consider dry; and adheres to Arminius, find those sermons livelier.

Thus, today, the major divisions in the African-American community are predominantly from four historically Black churches. Most are the Baptist (~64%), with six subdivisions, and the Pentecostals (~13%), with five subdivisions (Lugo et al., 2008). Followed by Methodist (~9%), with five subdivisions, and no division in the nonspecific Protestant church (~7%) (Lugo et al., 2008). Of the approximately 13% Pentecostals, 67% are from the COGIC church. The remaining 7% of historically Black churches closely affiliate with the Baptists or Pentecostals. The Lugo et al. (2008) survey captures the importance of religion for African-Americans:

> Of all the major racial and ethnic groups in the United States, Black Americans are the most likely to report a formal religious affiliation. Even among those Blacks who are unaffiliated, three-in-four belong to the "religious unaffiliated" category (that is, they say that religion is either somewhat or very important in their lives), compared with slightly more than one-third of the unaffiliated population overall.

The religious beliefs of the historically Black churches caused a division based on the strength of their adherence to Calvinism or Arminianism, but they united in the uniqueness of Afro-Theism developed during American slavery. Nevertheless, the divisions created the African-American subcultures like the COGIC church in this study. Therefore, the study is expanding Afro-Theism into a theoretical framework that incorporates an African-Americans' perspective of faith and social constructs, as seen in the next two sections. This understanding is an important part of the study's contribution to meeting the challenge of

18 Laying the Foundation

resolving the African-American diabetes epidemic (ADA, 2011; NDEP, 2011). That is, an effective discussion regarding diabetes education with these individuals requires an Afro-Theistic approach.

Afro-Theistic Faith

Afro-Theistic faith refers to African-Americans who go beyond believing in God to incorporating theism into their worldview or view of the world. Eltis' (2008) estimate of over 300 years since slavery began in North America, and lasting for more than 200 years, resulted in an Afro-Theistic inculcation of faith that compels African-Americans in defiance to observe and express it. Whether in the past, present, in politics or socially, a manifestation of overt expressions of their faith occurs and unavoidably influences decisions related to type 2 diabetes mellitus (T2DM). Examples of this expression of faith arose during the Texas State University's celebration of 50 years of integration. One of the five women interrupted the interview flow to let the audience know that all of them had a strong faith and community support that gave them the courage to do what they did (see Figure 3.1). Another example of this expression of faith emerged during the Phi Beta Sigma Fraternity's 100-year celebration when the speaker, a pastor, felt compelled to make his faith

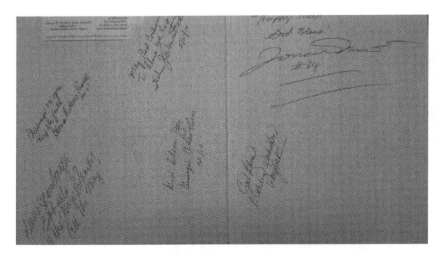

Figure 3.1 (A) Autographs of the first five African-Americans attending Texas State University celebrating 50 years of integration. From left-to-right and top-to-bottom on the left side: Gloria Odoms Powell, Helen Jackson Franks, Georgia Hoodye Cheatham, and Dana Jean Smith. At the bottom of the right side: Maybelline Washington Wozniak. (B) Autograph of the 34th Phi Beta Sigma Fraternity President: Celebrating 100 years - San Antonio Texas. The Honorable Jonathan A. Mason Sr.

known to the audience (see Figure 3.1). Undoubtedly, faith becomes a focal point of solidarity in subgroups, such as that of the COGIC.

All African-American religious or social groups have degrees of faith or beliefs that extend from their Afro-Theistic or spiritual constructs. Some of them, like the COGIC, piously reject assimilation into the White man's way of somber worship they see as extending from education and wealth (Hurston, 1981). However, Asante (1988) would classify COGIC piety as nothing more than the slave overseer's mentality. In other words, a mindset that believed that the slave could not be as good as their master and therefore seeks the master's approval to feel accepted. Hurston (1981) also noted that the most affluent African-Americans became, the more they assimilate into the White man's way of worship, which also should serve as a warning from Asante's perspective.

On the other hand, other African-Americans are faithful to Afrocentric philosophies and are more combative and also follow Thurman's purported definition of Black spirituality and critical race theory (Giles, 2010). Therefore, Afro-Theism includes Black spirituality, which stresses core social values, and critical race theory (CRT) that focuses on the ills of majoritarianism (majority decides). It also includes groups that have extremes of pacifism or fanaticism, the terms associated with COGIC (Weaver, 2003). Afro-Theism also recognizes other facets of CRT, like "racial formation," a term coined by Omi and Winant, that identifies the hegemony associated with that institution (2006). Afro-Theism also recognizes the fact that African-Americans may resort to any of these depending on the circumstance. However, it also includes groups that strongly object to engaging in temporal (worldly) social practices and have their particular brand of combativeness. Therefore, Afro-Theism acknowledges that many African-Americans have strong faiths that transcend temporal order and give priority to their eternal destiny while remaining Afrocentric. The COGIC church is in this group with a focus on eternity (Whitehead, 2001a) and adds another facet to their allegorical style of interpreting the Bible, further distinguishing it as a subculture.

Afro-Theistic faith in relationship to COGIC adult learners with T2DM focuses on diabetes educators and clinicians having confidence that these African-Americans will make the right decision when given adequate knowledge and respect for their faith. Therefore, with adequate knowledge and respect, these African-Americans will, on their initiative, obtain additional knowledge to manage their condition (Knowles, 1970). Knowles, Holton, and Swanson (2011) list characteristics of a "democratic" philosophy: conviction, faith, precedence, release, mutual trust, openness, attitude, and acceptance (Hansman & Mott, 2010; Knowles, 1970). Since African-Americans are next to the highest percentage per capita suffering from T2DM, this study looked for missing elements of democracy in the COGIC subculture related to their faith that hindered self-directed learning.

20 *Laying the Foundation*

Without this respect for the COGIC religion, equates to Knowles contrasting factors of paternalism, regimentation, restriction of information, suspicion, and forcing dependence upon authority. These hegemonic overtones can lead to deficit thinking, a term coined by scholars in the 1960s (Valencia, 1997), where, for example, critics would then blame COGIC members with diabetes for their condition. Unavoidably, the processes of adult learning involve social constructivism in relationship to Afro-Theism.

Afro-Theistic Constructivism

Afro-Theistic constructivism refers to meaning-making through African-American social influences as a means of learning (education) and survival. Individuals construct meaning based on observations in social settings rather than direct teachings. Historically, African-American adults forbid their children to join in conversations but overlook them if they were quiet. Therefore, African-American children practiced and mastered constructivism (meaning-making) early in life without knowing the terminology. The following is an example of a former slave, Amanda Smith (1837–1915):

> Then withal she was an earnest Christian, and had strong faith in God, as did also my grandmother. She was deeply pious, and a woman of marvelous faith and prayer. For the reason stated, my parents determined to move from Maryland, and so went to live on a farm owned by John Lowe, and situated on the Baltimore and York turnpike in the State of Pennsylvania.
>
> My father and mother both could read. But I never remember hearing them tell how they were taught. Father was the better reader of the two. Always on Sunday morning after breakfast, he would call us children around and read the Bible to us. I never knew him to sit down to a meal, no matter how scant, but what he would ask God's blessing before eating...
>
> (A. B. Smith, 1893, pp. 25–26)

Notice, as a child, Mrs. Smith learned by observing and not asking questions. This practice is still common in African-Americans' culture. Another example of Afro-Theistic constructivism in progress through the eyes of the researcher as an African-American child is brought to fruition in the following personal vignette.

> Papa, so named by all of his progenies, son of a former slave (Figure 3.2), a COGIC preacher, endured many prejudices without retaliation. However, it allowed seeing the polarity of racism in the 1960s, which likely makes it difficult for African-American diabetics

Afro-Theism: Subcultural Results 21

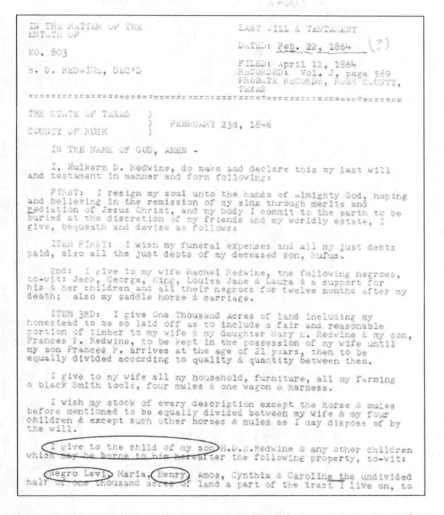

Figure 3.2 H. D. Redwine; Slave Owner's Will. Rusk County Court Record.

to trust outsiders. For example, as a preacher, he lived what he preached, by maintaining a friendship with White people, despite racism. "Colored" and "White" water and restrooms, is etched in memory as the only signs personally observed, paradoxically, at the place of justice, the county courthouse. Papa maintained a friendship with a cook at a hamburger joint but had to eat in a slightly filthy area behind the kitchen. Once, peeping around the corner and questioning why we could not set in the nicer area with the White people, resulted in a quick and forceful tug on the collar and him apologizing to the angry cook. The cook, in turn, apologized to the White patrons who overheard the conversations. The town had a segregated theater, but it did not matter since religious practices had prohibited patronage. There were some good results, like Papa's White friend inviting him to his house for dinner and the memorable experience with the first pork chop. On another occasion, another White man rigged a raffle to make certain Papa's son won a rocking chair.

Finally, the only memory of Jackie Robertson playing baseball is from Papa and his White friend that owned the furniture store in town, listening to baseball games on the radio. Papa, a fan, and an avid baseball player when he was younger; was proudly trying to convince his friend that Robinson was the greatest baseball player. Nevertheless, Papa was complicated. On the one hand, he questioned the desire to work for a White man since he refused, but enjoyed their friendship as an equal. On the contrary, he disagreed with Dr. Martin Luther King's leading of the Civil Rights marches, not because he did not see the social injustice, but because he thought a preacher should focus on saving souls. For him, the freedom to worship God in his Black religious way meant being a good representative of the cause of Christ as the primary concern above any other.

The previous conclusions are from Afro-Theistic constructivism, now believed and used to make inferences in social gatherings but based on observations without a discussion. Therefore, this Afro-Theistic study acknowledges that social cognition is the interaction of a three-way relationship between the COGIC members with diabetes, their religious environment that influences change, and their resulting behavior (Bandura, 1989; Davidson & Davidson, 2003). However, based on Black religion, the changes will include participants' effort to maintain their African heritage (Washington, 1964).

The social constructs of African-Americans began with slavery that initially imported only virulent young men, not fully indoctrinated in the African culture (Frazier, 1963). Furthermore, no more than five could congregate without a White man in the presence, which continued until introduced to the White man's religion (Frazier, 1963). These young men never fully gained the experiences of tribal customs, which made it easy to forget most of them. However, once allowed to assemble for religious purposes, the church became the means of all social activities that included music and the birth of Negro Spirituals, but sometimes carried secret messages. The "religion of Whites and the concern of the slaves were blended to create the Negro spirituals, which provided a cover for Negro preachers to lead insurrections and escape" (Washington, 1964). The customs born out of these assemblies became African-Americans' own "made in America" way of doing things. This idea of getting away to "do their own thing" is the social construct of the COGIC church.

Afro-Theistic constructivism also dictates the type of foods African-Americans enjoy. For example, Soul Food, which is uniquely African-American, is nothing more than taking whatever potentially consumable thing available and making it taste good. It usually means fatty, salty, and baked sweets. This way of eating was typical; they called it "making do." Making do was acceptable when resources were scarce, but this is not a sustainable diet today when more resources are available, and more inactivity from white collar jobs.

In conclusion, for many African-Americans, the most adhered source of social interactions is through one of the many social groups, primarily churches followed by other social organizations like fraternities and sororities (Davis, Clark, Carrese, Gary, & Cooper, 2005; Samad, 2013). The faith placed in the teachings of these groups often divides African-Americans into subcultures based on psychological or spiritual principles (Davis et al., 2005). This study focuses on one group to eliminate variables that would obscure the view of meaning-making. Investigated is the faith or convictions of the COGIC as a social group that governs or energizes the group through social interactions. Socialization then results as the premier source of influence for these individuals concerning the knowledge and interpretation of experiences with chronic diseases. Therefore, this study examines Afro-Theistic constructivism through the COGIC subculture of diabetic members beginning in the next chapter with personal reasons for selecting the COGIC subculture above others. It provides a historical look at the investigator's African-American and COGIC church background, providing additional understanding of Afro-Theism and the relationship between faith, knowledge, and the social constructs of the churches' members that led to the study's theoretical framework.

4 The COGIC Significant Subculture

The focus on African-Americans and type 2 diabetes mellitus (T2DM) emerged purely from a literature review of the disease. This emphasis evolved over four years, with two repeated themes: the prevalence of the disease in minority groups and the lack of African-Americans participating in support groups. While there were multiple types of diabetes, the most prevalent was T2DM. It usually surfaces in the late forties to midlife of an individual and its frequency varies within ethnic groups, but regardless, African-Americans were among the greatest number affected. Type 1 diabetes mellitus, which usually appears early in life, was second. Concerning coping with the disease, many studies, including Stockdale and Brockett, Taylor, and others, who based their works on Bandura's theories of self-efficacy, revealed the significance of emotional support developed in these groups. While participation in support groups seems like the best solution, the notion becomes complex when addressing traditionally closed groups like African-Americans per the research. The solution is complicated further when realizing that the African-American culture is subdivided based upon religious practices.

Ironically, the philosophy made of the beliefs and practices of these religious subgroups is how the African-American culture remains intact, though not by choice, but out of necessity. With such complexities, it should not be surprising that there is a dearth of research in developing a theory to explain such a far-reaching cultural phenomenon. That is, the causality and meaning of the subcultures, and the resulting philosophy's influence on health. It was this chasm or gaps in knowledge that brought to light that developing a theory could explain how the phenomena made of faith, knowledge, and social constructs have influenced the management of T2DM. To do so required the investigation of development of subcultures among African-Americans, lack of participation in support groups, and their perspective or thoughts related to T2DM. Being African-American with T2DM, an emerging researcher, a pastor, and a scientist whose teachings include T2DM and the need for a sustainable project seemed natural and obligatory to pursue to begin filling in these gaps of knowledge.

African-American Subcultures: Faith, Knowledge, and Social Constructs

Crucial in knowing that one could parse the African-American culture came from studies like Two Feathers (2005) who showed the reluctance of minority ethnic groups to participate in support groups, although African-Americans are far more reluctant to take part than Mexican-Americans, based on the numbers and number of groups found with these participants. Most significantly, the studies that did include African-Americans were almost exclusively faith-based. This discovery was crucial and resulted in an aha moment that shaped the course of this research. Concluding, there must be a connection between faith, African-Americans, and diabetes, since all three had impacted previous research findings. The result was an intense and desperate need to know "what was going on (Gaillard, 2007)" in the African-American culture with a notably lower life expectancy and them shunning help from support groups. Therefore, the search concerning T2DM branched into two categories: faith-based support and methodologies of a study best suited to understand the African-American culture, which eventually led to the grounded theory methodology.

However, initially came hints from the literature that a culture could be divided into subcultures when it suggested that certain identifiers transcended ethnicity. That is, although subcultures are divisions of a culture, as the name suggests, the most significant factor is what subcultures have in common, which transcends ethnicity. For instance, Jacobs citing Horton (2003) called the poor Whites in Appalachia a subculture of "the biggest gathering of poor White people in the United States (p. 12)," and considered them kindred to poor African-Americans, Indians, and Chicanos. In other words, the commonality being a poor American produced the subculture.

Therefore, and even more so, the Afro-Theistic nature of African-Americans required the recognition of their subcultural identifiers, faith, and social constructs as filters for their knowledge of T2DM. The idea of subcultural faith, knowledge, and social constructs builds upon Dewey's (1982) belief that all education comes from social consciousness in two forms: psychological (spirituality and faith) and sociological knowledge. The psychosocial nature of this study attempted to build on previous studies of African-American subcultures and T2DM.

Available research (Davis et al., 2005; Davis-Smith, 2007; Gaillard, 2007; Wade, 2005) primarily focused their studies on those in cultures most at risk. Therefore, most of the literature concerning diabetes also relates to African-Americans and Mexican-Americans, who have the highest incidence of diabetes. These studies also demonstrated a high correlation between spirituality and diabetes, especially in African-American women (Davis et al., 2005), who mostly adhere to their church culture. Equivalent spiritual mechanisms to cope and live with HIV (Baumgartner, 2000) infections came from partners who shared the experiences of those infected. In this vein, emotional support came through self-directed learning in social settings that empowered participants and practitioners to make changes (Baumgartner, 2011; Bricker et al., 2010; Kessler, Dubouloz, Urbanowski, & Egan, 2009). Nevertheless, studies like Gaillard (2007), Davis-Smith (2007), and Davis et al. (2005) agreed that the participants' faith, knowledge, and social constructs were vital parts of their lives when threatened by a disease. Thus, this magnified the demand for a theory grounded in data of how African-American subcultures' faith, knowledge, and social constructs work together, especially seeing these factors are more or less in place before the onset of the disease.

COGIC History and the Researcher

Efforts to gain the trust of African-Americans in knowledge and processes of managing chronic diseases like diabetes mellitus is most beneficial when endorsed by their social group, historically, their church affiliation. As will be elaborated, the reasons extend back to slavery, where the African-American culture uniquely merged with the church, but it also divided them into subcultures. Therefore, since each church denomination represents a separate subculture, selecting one representative group removed variables that would interfere with developing a theory related to the knowledge of T2DM. As a researcher, the choice of the church denominations extended from familiarity. As a result, this study focused on the Church of God in Christ denomination that influences the decision-making processes of its members, from which the researcher is also an ordained elder. The Church of God in Christ or COGIC, pronounced Cō-jic, began during a critical theological and pedagogical juncture in the American history. That is, during the first shifts from an emphasis on traditional educational institutes such as the family, church, and schools toward the priority of the industrial workplaces (Enns, 1989; Kasworm, Rose, & Ross-Gordon, 2010). This transition was during the late 1800s when America had moved from colonialism into the prosperous industrial age. In 1859, former seminarian Charles Darwin wrote a book called *The Origin of Species*, whose application made an indelible impact on the traditional interpretation of biblical scriptures and initiated relativism "in the guise of biblical criticism" (Brown, 1995, p. 554). Consequently, it challenged many conservative theological views and promoted liberal (feeling) theology traceable back to Friedrich Schleiermacher (1763–1834), and infiltrated Christian seminaries (Enns, 1989). During this time, African-Americans, more than 90% of which lived in the South (Bureau, 2002a, 2002b), were also trying to find their place as postslavery citizens.

The researcher's historical background lies in a prominent Southern African-American family. Nevertheless, his ancestors were ex-slaves, typical of those in the South who suffered many injustices. As seen in Figure 3.2, in 1864, H. D. Redwine willed his slaves Levi (1831–1895), the researcher's great-grandfather, and Henry (1853–1930), his grandfather, to H. D.'s children. However, the Emancipation Proclamation of January 1, 1863, had occurred over one year prior. Allegedly, Texas "got the news" on June 19, 1865, although H. D. Redwine's son Hullum Duke Erasmus was a Confederate cavalry officer (see: http://www.tshaonline.org/handbook/online/articles/fre70). Eventually, Grandpa Henry inherited 1,000 acres, owned a cotton gin, employed laborers, and purportedly owned the first tractor in his East Texas area. According to Papa, when Henry died, Banks took the five hundred (500) acres that he had put up for collateral on that tractor. When asked why Papa and his siblings did not just pay the loan off, he said, "they wu'en let us." Currently, the descendants of Papa, Fernander (1888–1985), are one of only three descendants of Levi who own their entire 50 acres.

The slow traveling news of the emancipation reveals the antiassimilationist white South's attitude toward African-Americans and the influential whites pushing back after losing the Civil War with laws to prevent leveling (Samad, 2013). Most African-Americans were poor and uneducated, making them easy targets of racial prejudice. In the real sense of the term bricolage of resources (Crotty, 1998), to survive, African-Americans had to "make-do" with whatever was available, including medical care. This type of survival strategy was the case as late as the 1960s. For example, all 19 of the researcher's siblings were born at home except one, and somehow, the clinicians were not able to prevent the navel cord from choking Gayla Masha to death. They returned to birthing children at home for the last siblings. Another example is the severe laceration the researcher received that ran from the bottom of the sternum to the navel—a foot cut in half by a broken mason jar and suffering a severe burn after chasing a toy into a wood stove, all treated with home remedies and prayer.

Likewise, churches played a vital role in former slaves' survival both physically and educationally, where clergymen usually were the most educated in the African-American community, and the church was generally a haven from physical violence (Giles, 2010; Weaver, 2003). The founder of the COGIC denomination was Charles Harrison Mason, a contemporary of Papa, though older, but both were born not too long postslavery. However, Mason the elder was born in 1864, the year following the emancipation, but suffered the injustices of the reconstruction as seen in 1866 on Mr. John Watson's Plantation in Bartlett Tennessee. His parents were Jeremiah and Eliza Mason, and her conversion (accepting Christ as Lord and Savior) came during slavery at the Missionary Baptist Church (Brown, 1995; Whitehead, 2001a). His dad could not afford

Charles the time for education, but being a precocious child, his mind blossomed with imagination in the fashion of Maxine Greene (1995) into what he called visions, from biblical stories. Notably, documents state that the church's name came to him as he was pondering in 1897. He said, "God spoke to him out of 1 Thessalonians 2:14...the churches of God which in Judea are in Christ" (Whitehead, 2001a, p. 9). In the meantime, Mason's conversion came at the age of 12, and then at 14, he became deathly ill in 1880. His mother was devout and known as one of great faith and prayer, and on the first Sunday that September, Mason received what he described as miraculous healing. This idea of receiving miraculous healing became a key feature of faith within the COGIC denomination.

The remaining steps in the evolution of the COGIC denomination are a combination of ontologies (Kincheloe & McLaren, 2008) that were countercultural to both White Americans and African-Americans of those times. Mason's baptism came from the hands of his brother at Mt. Olive Baptist Missionary Church, near Plumerville, Arkansas. "Bishop Mason dedicated his entire life to preserving one thing—the spiritual essence of the Black religious experience and the prayer tradition that those old slaves had back in the brush arbors" (Whitehead, 2001a, p. 7). His love for the Bible is in opposition to Cremin's premise that the "whip and the Bible" were the pedagogies to keep Blacks in a White version of their existence. Instead, it reflects a second pedagogy premise that "through family and clandestine religious assembly," African-Americans maintained their identity (Kasworm et al., 2010, p. 89). The phrase "whip in the Bible" was from Giles (2010) book that tells of an incident with an influential African-American named Howard Thurman. Thurman's grandmother taught him based on her experiences of seeing a White preacher who would embellish the writings of Paul, the apostle where he admonished slaves to obey their masters. Although his grandmother would balance these teachings with a slave circuit minister who "reminded them that they were not niggers nor slaves, but God's children," yet, she forbid her grandson to read the Pauline letters (Giles, 2010, p. 336).

Other churches, like the COGIC members, just did not believe everything people said, as evident when Mason rejected the teachings of C. L. Fisher, the academic dean of the newly founded Arkansas Baptist College, and an Arkansas Baptist Convention leader. Fisher was a Greek and Latin scholar who graduated from Morgan Park Seminary in Illinois, now called the University of Chicago Divinity School. Although Fisher, A. M. Booker (Arkansas Baptist College president) and his wife took Mason in as a son, he rejected their way of biblical interpretation called higher criticism. He believed he could do a better job with the Bible and prayer alone. This example later became another fundamental feature of the COGIC denomination, where minister (men) and missionary (women) licenses came from their felt inspiration by the Holy Spirit to preach and teach, unlike other denominations that primarily qualify individuals based upon their education.

After Mason had acknowledged his conviction to preach, he preached his first message based on the autobiography of Amanda Smith (1837–1915), known as the greatest Black evangelist of the nineteenth century. This willingness to follow women's teachings led to another fundamental countercultural feature of the COGIC denomination where women then and now participate in ministry equally with men, up to the point of being an ordained minister. C. P. Jones worked alongside Mason, and they extracted from the Scripture the idea of living holy, which was countercultural to what they were observing. In 1895, C. P. Jones attended the Baptist Convention in Salem, Alabama, and became disappointed with the convention's focus:

> Because while they [Baptist] were concerned about the racism in America, the political disfranchisement of Blacks and the great dehumanization process that was going on in America, they organized but were not putting much emphasis on the spiritual element in the Black religious experience. They were putting the emphasis on the social side, on the political side, and on the educational side, but were putting no emphasis on the spiritual needs.
> (Whitehead, 2001a, p. 9)

Holiness, the idea of living free from sin through sanctification, became another fundamental feature of the church, but this teaching caused fights within the Baptist Church, and in 1896, those who believed this teaching were disenfranchised (Whitehead, 2001a). This countercultural belief is yet another fundamental feature of this church since it chooses to hear messages that emphasize living a spiritual life versus the entanglement in current events. This countercultural praxis led to another fundamental feature of this church, in that it has openly embraced all races even during the time of segregation. Blacks and Whites often secretly fellowship together during this dangerous time.

Later, when the number of Whites, who served under Bishop Mason, grew in numbers, the elders asked Mason for his blessing to divide into a separate denomination, presumably from racist pressure during that time. Consequently, Bishop Mason, after ordaining many White ministers over previous years, agreed, and some of these men started the Pentecostal "Assemblies of God" (Weaver, 2003). Sadly, Mason and his COGIC choir were the only two African-American churches invited to their inaugural Hot Springs Convention in 1914 (Weaver, 2003).

Weaver (2003, p. 49) states, "David Daniels says the early interracial impetus existing in COGIC has been neglected, Mason's contribution to the interracial impulse within Pentecostalism and American

Protestantism remains an understudied topic of American religious history." For example, when the American South condemned interracial gatherings, the predominantly African-American COGIC church crossed racial barriers and welcomed fellowship with Whites. In other instances, they welcomed a Baptist minister, Dr. Martin Luther King, at Mason Temple COGIC in Memphis, Tennessee, when he was receiving his worse criticism. Finally, Faith Temple COGIC in Harlem, New York, permitted Malcolm X's funeral when others would not. However, COGIC has several dogmas of which many Evangelicals disagree, such as "...their emphasis upon healing, gifts of prophecy, speaking-in-tongues, spirit possession, and religious dance" (Weaver, 2003, p. 35). Notably, the conviction that all believers must "speak in tongues" that came after Mason's Los Angeles visit with Elder William Joseph Seymour and the Azusa Street revival caused Mason and C. P. Jones to part ways. Upon the return from the Azusa Street revival, Mason conducted meetings (revivals) that had thousands of converts (African-American and White) to the new belief. The Memphis Commercial Appeal published the following:

> Fanatical worship of Negroes going on at Sanctified Church... Strange things have been going on at this [COGIC] church...and if the authorities do not interfere some lives are sure to be sacrificed to the fanatical spirit which has been controlling the church for the last month.
> (Weaver, 2003, p. 45)

Admittedly, COGIC does have core dogmas, but there is flexibility since each pastor interprets these meanings based upon their spiritual convictions. The previously mentioned cases of helping non-membered leaders are examples of flexibility since the church as an organization did not vote on those decisions. Although many COGIC leaders did not agree, a few used their liberty to act according to their conviction. As a result, members of local churchgoers' understanding of church dogmas come from Bible studies and pastor (primarily) or ministers speaking to the congregation. In comparison to for-profit businesses, most assemblies are independently owned franchises that submit to cooperate rules with privileges to carry the incorporated logo.

However, pastors must first become elders through ordination before establishing or receiving an appointment to the pastorate. This process usually takes years of faithfully serving under a pastor as a member, and then as a minister, which is efficient in weeding out those who do not qualify based upon core beliefs. The organization maintains the unity through an annual fall pilgrimage to a Holy Convocation, held for many years in Memphis, Tennessee. Historically, the timing allowed its members, nearly all farmers located throughout the United States, time to gather and sell their crops to have the money to make the trip.

Increasingly, COGIC is developing its curriculum to educate its ministers and missionaries. However, Mason recognized the need to educate its youth from the beginning and developed educational schools and curricula, but the education stressed godliness and holiness (Whitehead, 2001b). Over the years through the education of younger leaders and the death of elders, COGIC leadership has relaxed some of its former extreme views. For example, deferring to conscientious objection in wartimes, the notion that it is a sin to go to the movies, or even sporting events has changed. The extreme view of some preachers that watching television was a sinful endeavor has all but disappeared.

Slowly through education over time, change has occurred in this austere subculture of African-Americans and gives reason to believe that diabetes education is beneficial. However, it also highlights the importance of knowing how these learn to change, or what causes African-Americans to change. Therefore, it seemed best to limit the number of variables to the education of one subculture and then develop a theory grounded in these participants' data that teased out their relationship to our understanding of diabetes, continued in Part 2. That is, letting the voice of COGIC members with T2DM informs the theory developed, with the desired effect of opening the door to understanding how all African-Americans and perhaps beyond this ethnic group cope with this and other chronic diseases. Part 2 provides the rationale for the study based on the research questions and the methodology.

Part 2
Research Approach

After previously establishing the benefits of grounded theory, Part 2 continues by discussing the problem in Chapter 5 and developing the research questions. In Chapter 6, grounded theory prevailed as the means of providing an approach that promised to meet the challenges of representing a diverse culture of African-Americans while suggesting ways to effect change in the lives of those with type 2 diabetes mellitus (T2DM). Finally, Chapter 7 gives full disclosure of the origin and benefits of the grounded theory methodology. Part 2 is essential in justifying the need for a theory grounded in the data of the subcultures and allowing the hypothesis to develop (Fraenkel, Wallen, & Hyun, 2012) from the theory.

5 So, What Is the Problem?

There is a systemic lack of diabetes support in the African-American diabetic community due to nonparticipation from fear of those with resources even in as simple as diabetes education because those empowered do not understand the culture. For this reason, those willing to help with education and financial resources rely on church-based organizations since most African-Americans have a church affiliation. From the literature, the problem with church-based organizations in the African-American community is twofold. First, understandably, church-based support groups operate ad hoc within the constraints of time and resources. Moreover, missing in the research is the benefit of having a theory grounded in the voices of African-Americans that would help facilitate changes based on principles of respecting them as responsible adults. For this reason, the grounded theory methodology became the choice, since it uses the researcher, to empower the participants in developing a model catered to them.

Second, relatively few churches take advantage of the chances available to help those with diabetes because that is not the primary function of a church and the relative few with the knowledge or the priority of tracking short-lived opportunities. The result is a decrease in support for the African-American culture that prolongs suffering and with the potential for continued distress to the economy. Therefore, the development of a theory grounded in the participants' data to encourage more support was needed but required an investigation to demystify the reasons for the church affiliation of many African-Americans in the first place.

Church-based support rightfully suggests a sharp division of the African-American culture into socially based subcultures. The reason for these divisions is church denominations, such as the Church of God in Christ (COGIC) used in this study. Each African-American denomination or religious organization has beliefs that divide the community and need an understanding of how they relate to type 2 diabetes mellitus (T2DM). Familiarity with the COGIC church helps in providing details of a significant population of African-Americans.

Historically, those associated with the COGIC denomination have received double marginalization due to their assertive and dogmatic style of preaching the gospel (Range, Young, Ross, & Winbush, 1973). This marginalization extends from its African-American founding and fundamental beliefs in Holiness and in living by faith. However, this marginalized African-American Holiness group is 6.5 million worldwide and 5.5 million in America (Houdmann, 2012), making this a foundational manuscript for African-Americans from an African-American researcher. Two Feathers (2005) indicates that faith-based support groups are the best means of helping many in the African-American and Mexican-American communities learn about, cope with, and adjust to life as a person with diabetes. In recognition of the benefits of faith-based support, the American Diabetes Association (ADA, 2013) developed programs like Project Power for African-American churches to manage diabetes.

However, the COGIC church has other beliefs, like divine healing as in the days of the apostles of Christ, which further distinguishes them as a unique African-American subculture (Range et al., 1973). The COGIC church's uniqueness has resulted in the marginalization that makes members reluctant to participate in support groups.

The COGIC church's marginalization began with physical violence of gunfire at the church's founding in 1897. Disgruntled shooters fired five shots from multiple guns into the crowd of worshipers during its second revival (Range et al., 1973). Preceding this attack, the Baptist Church denomination in 1896 ordered its doors close to the teachings of the founder and his followers (Range et al., 1973). Ironically, another marginalized individual named Martin Luther King Jr. (Estate of Dr. Martin Luther King Jr., n.d.), a Baptist preacher preached his last and famous "I've Been to the Mountaintop" message in the COGIC headquarters, in Memphis Tennessee. In this vein, Boucouvalas and Lawrence (2010) argue that every person is a product of their multiple identifications imposed upon them by systems in which they participate. COGIC members' multiple identifications come from marginalization or "othered" (Charmaz, 2011, p. 371) as African-Americans, marginalization as a church denomination, and marginalization as strong believers in living by faith.

The COGIC church is a humble, sacrificial, and relatively private African-American subculture. Traditionally, church attendance, biblical living, and emphases on the eternal order of heaven have prominence over temporal affairs on earth. One example is fasting, which traditionally meant refraining from eating food or drinking water for hours or even days. In the place of food and water, members pray to God while continuing to engage in daily activities without anyone knowing.

Fasting poses a problem when it comes to diseases such as T2DM, where clinicians expect these patients to eat smaller portions six times a day while continuing to take the regimented dosages of medication. Discussing fasting with a doctor is unheard of due to ethnic differences.

Even with African-American physicians, the chance of them being Pentecostals is small. The risk of appearing ignorant or disgracing African-Americans is a constant worry. The conclusion is that doctors do not know of these cultural practices; if so, they certainly do not let patients know. The fear of negative feedback prevents African-Americans from discussing T2DM with clinicians, especially the COGIC subculture that believes in divine healing. COGIC diabetic adults accept the problems as their fate in this life and manage it in private in the best manner possible. However, marginalization is avoidable with a theory grounded in data that brings an understanding of this subculture. Having knowledge of this subculture in relationship to diabetes will eventually erode the reluctance of COGIC church members accessing resources to help themselves by developing and participating in an African-American support group.

This summation is rooted in an adult education theory that facilitates understanding of COGIC diabetic members, with an added potential of affecting the economy through changes they make. Already, as reflected in the interviews, many in the African-American community feel the medical community thinks they will eventually develop diabetes. Such thinking gives the impression that African-Americans are the cause of increased medical expenses in the United States. Even if that was true, and it is not, a theory grounded in the interviews of African-Americans invites opportunities for discussions leading to changes.

For clarification, and to erase the negative impressions in the minds of many African-Americans, the number per capita with T2DM is consistent with a population's percentage. Meaning, ethnic groups with the greatest number in the population has the largest number of citizens with T2DM. What is disproportionate is the rate per capita in each ethnic group. For example, combining 2010 census statistics, Table 5.1 shows that the actual number of African-Americans with T2DM is next to last, but have almost the greatest percentage of its ethnic group affected (CDC, 2012a; Ennis,

Table 5.1 National Diabetes Statistics by Ethnicity

Ancestry	Population Percentage	Population* (million)	Percentage with Diabetes	Number with Diabetes (million)
White Americans	72.4	224	7.6	17.0
Hispanic or Latino	16.3	50	12.8	6.4
African-American	12.6	39	13.2	5.1
American Indians & Alaskan Natives	0.9	3	15.9	0.5

* Based on the total population of 309 million rounded to the nearest million. 2010 Census.

Ríos-Vargas, & Albert, 2011; Hixson, Hepler, & Kim, 2011; Norris, Vines, & Hoeffel, 2012; Rastogi, Johnson, Hoeffel, & Drewery, 2011).

Although the statistics show that the number of African-Americans with T2DM is next to last, they also revealed that the opposite is true, that is, they are placed second in terms of the greatest percentage of the ethnic groups affected.

Therefore, these statistics reveal the urgent need for African-Americans to have dialogues concerning reversing this trend. However, the dialogue needs a point of reference that is uniquely African-American. The development of a theory grounded in the data of diabetic adults in the COGIC subculture provides an initial reference for dialogue. To date, the chance to dialogue about T2DM in the African-American community is small since there are relatively few support groups for this culture. As an example, of the two support groups discovered within the region, Hispanics facilitated both, and though open to the public, the audience was predominantly from the same culture. One of the two diabetes educators demonstrated the importance of exclusivity in the Hispanic and African-American support groups when clients detected subtle differences between them; he told them he was a South American. Thus, with personal discussions on issues of diabetes, two things essential to participants become apparent: the importance of cultural exclusivity, and cultural knowledge. Upon further investigation, the only local African-American support groups were sporadic forms of church-based short-termed programs facilitated by pastors.

The observation of church-based local support served as another reminder that African-Americans have subcultures based on religious practices. Without in-depth knowledge of the subculture, facilitators have little chance of helping those with an already small support structure. The fact that research such as Two Feathers (2005) reveals church-based support groups as working best for African-Americans gives evidence that there is a gap in knowledge about this culture. A theory grounded in the data of diabetic adults in an African-American faith-based subculture provides a platform for diabetes educators to communicate with the culture.

African-Americans, based on the latest census (2010), statistically are among the greatest percentage per capita of those living below the poverty level (DeNavas-Walt, Proctor, & Smith, 2011). Poverty warrants further considerations based on a collaborative initiative between "faith-based health advocates, lay church members (facilitated by Interfaith Partnership's Abraham's Children), and academics that began in 1999 in St. Louis, Mo" (Baker et al., 2006). The intervention program that started in 1999 continued through the publication of the peer-reviewed journal article in 2006. Baker et al. (2006) found social and environmental factors that significantly influenced the eating behaviors of African-Americans in St. Louis, Missouri. For example, socially, they found that in low-income and minority neighborhoods, grocery stores have fewer healthy choices for shoppers that led to obesity, a contributing factor to diabetes.

Environmentally, they observed that the transportation systems in these neighborhoods influenced a community's level of obesity. Therefore, according to the 2010 census, the COGIC African-American diabetic communities in this study have the same obstacles to making healthy choices. Also, Baker et al. (2006) noted that other intervention studies focused on two aspects of obesity—eating habits and physical activity—while ignoring social and environmental causes. Additionally, Baker et al.'s (2006) intervention magnifies the importance of developing a theory for a better understanding of diabetes from the African-Americans perspective. This development requires beginning with one subculture of African-Americans divided by Afro-Theistic beliefs.

The statistics in Table 5.1 reveal the reason the COGIC church is the Afro-Theistic subculture in this study. In comparison, the COGIC membership alone outnumbers the entire population of Native Americans and Alaska Natives who are the largest percentage affected by T2DM. The COGIC fervent belief in divine healing by faith makes them an easy target for marginalization because of their Afro-Theist faith. Therefore, discovering how they process knowledge of diabetes using their data show the COGIC members with T2DM respect and give them a reason to trust that their participation in a faith-based support group is for their benefit. Two Feathers (2005) and Ruder, Blank, Hale, Nienow, and Rollins (2007) show that an understanding of a subculture helps them build the trust in the process and gives them the space required to self-identify conflicts.

These moments of discovery is what Brazilian philosopher and educator Freire called "conscientization" (1998). The self-identity facilitates the American philosopher and educator Horton as cited by Jacob (2003) belief that ethnic members should take responsibility to solve their problems in conjunction with available help. To promote this democratic process, also called the relocation of power (Cornwall & Jewkes, 1995), a theory grounded in the data of people with diabetes with fervent convictions of Afro-Theist faith is essential. Moreover, a theory grounded in the data of this admittedly dogmatic (Range et al., 1973). The Afro-Theistic subculture provides a model for studies of less dogmatic Afro-Theistic subcultures. With an understanding of the problem, and having chosen a group for the study, the next chapter focuses on the purpose, questions, and the grounded theory methodology.

6 Purpose and Questions

Purpose of the Study

This study developed a theory grounded in data of how Church of God in Christ (COGIC) members with diabetes combine their Afro-Theistic faith with their knowledge of type 2 diabetes mellitus (T2DM), through Afro-Theistic social constructs. The theory is for understanding this Afro-Theist subculture of COGIC members' efforts to manage T2DM and provide an instrument to oppose the current trend of diabetes in African-Americans. Missing in the African-American diabetic community is a theory that inquires about the problems of diabetes for a supportive and collaborative effort to promote healthy living that supplants the desires for isolation. Although support groups appear to be the best means of diabetes maintenance in the African-American population, there is another previously mentioned crucial consideration for this populous. This culture has multiple unique subcultures within it.

The many subcultures primarily resulted from religious differences; a significant polarization is the 5.5 million members of the COGIC denomination (Grissom-II, 2013; Houdmann, 2012; U.S. Census Bureau, 2012; Waldron, 2008). This polarization resulted from "dogmatic" (Range et al., 1973, p. 25) spiritual convictions that marginalize them in the eyes of other African-American religious groups. For this reason, it is necessary to understand how people with diabetes in this subculture reconcile their faith with diabetes education through their social constructs before an invitation to a support group. The understanding of this subculture helps in the design of a support group by considering the affected adult's age, years living with the disease, and other findings that help facilitate changes.

Already known is that knowledge about diabetes, self-management, and short-term intervention does not provide sufficient long-term changes in the management of diabetes (Saydah, Fradkin, & Cowie, 2004; Two Feathers, 2005; Williams, Manias, Liew, Gock, & Gorelik, 2012). Thus, having a theory grounded in the data of this culture helps to build a sustainable diabetes support group with long-term benefits for the community of African-Americans with diabetes (Baker et al., 2006).

Finally, Kuhn's (1999) critical thinking through action and reflection on those activities is necessarily part of managing diabetes in the COGIC subculture. However, for sustainability through support groups, this study develops a theory grounded in data that combine Afro-Theistic faith, knowledge about diabetes, and Afro-Theistic social constructs.

Research Questions

The grounded theory developed came from one guiding question in mind: "What are the processes involved when COGIC members with type 2 diabetes mellitus (T2DM) construct knowledge about the disease through their Afro-Theistic faith and Afro-Theistic social constructs?" Asking the following questions was the means of ascertaining the information to develop the theory grounded in data of the participants:

1   What does diabetes education look like for the Afro-Theistic COGIC diabetes mellitus sufferers?
2   How can Afro-Theistic faith and diabetes education coexist to help T2DM sufferers?
3   What are diabetic COGIC members' Afro-Theistic social constructs' beliefs about diabetes mellitus?
    - What are the Afro-Theistic social constructs?
4   How does the Afro-Theistic social constructs' interpretation of diabetes mellitus, overtly, or covertly influence COGIC member's resolve to disregard intervention?

Although not one of the questions, of interest was a better understanding of individuals that researcher identified as having a "martyr response" to the disease. Nonetheless, these research questions required a personal understanding of African-Americans, and this required a knowledge of the Theism that divides African-Americans into subcultures.

Answers to the research questions provide a qualitative approach to help African-Americans have space to self-identify means and obstacles to managing diabetes. Management is especially important since the American Diabetes Association (ADA) lists diabetes as the seventh leading cause of death in America. Additionally, the Centers for Disease Control and Prevention (2011), diabetes has maintained that status for several years. Also, there exists a relationship between diabetes and coronary heart disease (CHD), the number one killer in America. CHD is one of the many complications associated with T2DM (ADA, 2011; Roger et al., 2010). Currently, 18.7% of African-Americans (NDEP, 2011) and more than 7% of the American population (Davis-Smith, 2007) are diabetic with no sign of decreasing. The fact is the ADA predicts that one in three Americans will suffer from T2DM by 2050. However, the prospects are even more abysmal for African-Americans and Mexican-Americans. Today one in three of them are predicted to develop T2DM within their lifetime (ACS, ADA, AHS, & ASA, 2011; Roger et al., 2010). In other words, within the life of all African-Americans and Mexican-Americans presently living, more than 33% will develop T2DM.

Missing are the qualitative studies of African-Americans that approach the problem from their perspective. This qualitative study included research questions necessary to develop a theory grounded in the data of African-Americans from their theistic perspective. For this reason, answering the research questions for African-Americans also addresses multifaceted problems with T2DM. These problems involve not only the individual but also American society when considering the rising cost of health care (ACS et al., 2011). Diabetes-related expenses accrue directly in the form of kidney diseases and its complications that can result in renal (kidney) failure and the need for a kidney transplant. Diabetes indirectly accrues costs in the form of heart disease and stroke, high blood pressure, nervous system disease, and amputations. Added to the conundrum is that the exact cause of T2DM has yet to be determined (ADA, 2011), despite knowing that genetics and the environment are contributing factors. Regardless of what causes diabetes, doctors and the federal government welcome partners to reverse these trends and bring the disease under control. Therefore, the government initiated "The Catalyst to Better Diabetes Care Act of 2009, which is part of the Patient Protection and Affordable Care Act" (CDC, 2012a).

A term that indicated change and popularized by Adult Educator Jack Mezirow (1991) is transformational learning. Mezirow (1991) explains that adults have lifelong learning experiences that give them a "frame of reference." For transformation or change to occur, it requires a "disorienting dilemma or personal crisis" (Baumgartner, 2000; Mezirow, 1991). In this vein, there are a wealth of quantitative data and governmental intervention programs (CDC, 2012b) focusing on evidence-based lifestyle changes, leading to the prevention and treatment of T2DM medically. An Afro-Theistic theory grounded in the data of the COGIC members with T2DM based on the research questions provides the missing knowledge needed in the African-American community. Many researchers indicate the need for answers. Most relative is Melancon, Oomen-Early, and del Rincon (2009) and Two Feathers (2005) mixed-method studies.

Also important are Davis-Smith's (2007) mixed-method study and Ntiri and Stewart's (2009) quantitative research. These gave evidence that intervention groups promote self-directed learning that results in transformational learning. The promising evidence ranged from the reduction of diabetes complications to the prevention of T2DM in prediabetics, which accounts for 90–95% of all diabetes. Also, an article by Gaillard (2007) that stressed the importance of faith-based subcultures in diabetes management corroborated these findings. Furthermore, these studies, especially Two Feathers (2005), revealed the importance of cultural exclusiveness as a vital factor that leads to transformation. If the culture requires exclusiveness for changes to occur, then it makes sense to consider a large subcultural segment that potentially impedes the desired effects of diabetes maintenance. COGIC is a large body of Afro-Theistic African-Americans that is unique in their beliefs in living by faith. This peculiarity makes them a subculture with views paradoxical to diabetes education. This denomination consists of 5.5 of the 42 million African-Americans; this is more than 13%, and, therefore, a significant population to consider supporting to reverse the trend of diabetes in the African-American community.

Because of the gap in qualitative research, a theory focused on how Afro-Theistic subcultures reconcile faith with diabetes education through social constructs does not exist. Conversely, this lack of theory with "exclusivity" about the African-American culture promoted this gap in understanding. In Part 6, the findings give plausible explanations to the questions related to the socially constructed meaning of diabetes through Afro-Theistic faith, the diabetes education of the COGIC T2DM sufferers, and how they juxtaposition the two in managing the disease. However, the immediate need is the more in-depth understanding of grounded theory found in Chapter 7.

7 Qualitative Research
Grounded Theory

Merriam (2009) notes that qualitative research began as a concept with anthropologist and sociologist inquiry of "people's lives, the social and cultural contexts in which they lived, the ways in which they understood their worlds, and so on" (p. 6). Bogdan and Biklen (2007) further claimed these Chicago School socialists used qualitative research to give voice to those marginalized in society. In this study, African-Americans, specifically COGIC members with diabetes, are the ones that need their voice heard. Typical, no hypothesis exists; instead, there is a need to build a relationship with the participants and let the hypothesis "emerge as a study progresses" (Fraenkel et al., 2012, p. 86). Doing so allows this qualitative study to help others assist African-Americans with diabetes combine their subcultural faith-based practices with diabetes education, which increases the opportunities for more support.

By force of will were constant reminders that the ultimate goal is to bring understanding and support to the African-American community of people living with diabetes. The idea of studying one subculture of African-Americans also follows Cordova's (2011) seventh recommendation to explore the "Spiritual culture of one ethnic group of type 2 diabetic patients." Limiting participation to one subculture of African-Americans with T2DM gives recognition that such divisions exist and equates to ethnic respect as adult learners.

Furthermore, an inductive study of one subculture helps track their meaning-making based on their knowledge of T2DM when filtered through their faith-based practices and social constructs. In other words, the exclusivity to African-Americans makes this study one that lays the foundation for others to build on. Specifically, the selection of the COGIC subculture empowered them through the voices of individuals with T2DM, which was used to discover how their knowledge about diabetes merges with faith through their social constructs. This understanding not only assists this subculture in transforming their lives to manage the disease but also serves as a model for other African-American subcultures to follow in doing the same. Equally, understanding this subculture helps those outside the culture assist in reversing the spread of diabetes in the African-American community.

Likewise, this understanding serves as a model to investigate non-African-American cultures with strong beliefs built into their social constructs. The overall objective is to understand how a significantly large subculture in the African-American society reconciles their knowledge of T2DM with their faith-based practices to manage the disease. Therefore, through grounded theory, whose application closes the chapter of this book, reflects a qualitative study that explains how the social constructs of one African-American subculture combined faith and T2DM knowledge, ultimately hoping to help prevent and reverse the effects, or manage diabetes.

Grounded Theory Methodology

This grounded theory study builds upon its current use with Afro-Theism while keeping the discoverers', Glaser and Strauss (1967), original understanding as the central focus. A grounded theory does not compete with other theories but differs in that hypotheses, categories, and, finally, a theory emerges from the collected data from the participants. In other words, a theory develops grounded in the data from the participants.

When introduced, the originators believed that their research colleagues would only consider grounded theory as a hypothesis (Glaser & Strauss, 1967). Since then, grounded theory has matured into a sustainable methodology and continues to evolve, and lately, used for means other than generating a theory (Corbin & Strauss, 2007). Multiple users of grounded theory as a descriptive methodology caused Corbin, a fellow researcher with Strauss, to broaden the definition to Glaser and Strauss' inclusion while developing the theory. They acknowledge grounded theory as a methodology "in a more generic sense to denote theoretical construct derived from qualitative analysis of data" (Corbin & Strauss, 2007, p. 1). Meaning the general definition concedes to the possibility of using the methodology for means other than building a theory. The eclectic use of the theory resulted from Taylor (2010) and Kessler et al. (2009), with the grounded theory methodology used in a similar manner of Crotty's (1998) reference to ethnography. He said, "grounded theory can be viewed as a particular form of ethnographic inquiry that, through a series of carefully planned steps, develops theoretical ideas" (Crotty, 1998, p. 78), with an emphasis on the idea, rather than a theory.

However, most use grounded theory for its original intent of producing a theory, especially those in the medical field (Corbin & Strauss, 2007). The association between grounded theory and the medical field is the theory's development "was made possible by Public Health Service Research Grant NU-0047 from the Division of Nursing, Bureau of State Services-Community Health" (Glaser & Strauss, 1967, p. ix). Reflecting on Strauss and Corbin's definition, Taylor (2010) stated that grounded theory is "a theory that is derived from data, systematically gathered and analyzed through the research process. The researcher begins with an area of study and allows the theory to emerge from the data" (p. 10). The source of data varied; one was in the form of interviews (Rohde, 2010), while Baumgartner's (2011) meta-analysis built on the research of others. Taylor (2010) modified a previously validated questionnaire called the Godin Leisure-Time Exercise Questionnaire (GLTEQ).

All these models of grounded theory inquiry purposefully included the voice of the patients and sometimes the practitioners. A relevant, older example used focus groups to understand an eclectic mixture of caregivers and those with various chronic diseases, including diabetes (Maine State Dept. of Human Services, 1997). From this report emerged actions and processes salient to adult education and this study (Charmaz, 2011). Central to the findings was the sufferers who expressed the need for others to hear them concerning the positive and negative impact of caregivers. Chronic sufferers expressed anxiety about health insurance and health care and the need for caregivers to recognize the importance of their role in living healthy.

Regardless of the approach, the advantage of grounded theory is its ability to generate a theory to explain phenomena based on an in-depth analysis of the empirical evidence of the participants. As a result, the generation of theory provides vital information for caregivers to understand their patients better and knowing how to help them manage chronic diseases. For example, in his mixed-method study, Taylor (2010) assembled a group with similar conditions and used grounded theory methodologies to analyze surveys containing the opinions of health professionals ($n = 20$) and adults ($n = 12$). The theory helped medical personnel gain an understanding of their patients, which enabled them to provide better care. From this small sample size used to develop a grounded theory, he then surveyed 232 prediabetics over three subsequent studies to complete a quantitative study, to optimize the findings in support of diabetes sufferers' needs.

Notably, germane to the initial discovery is a focus on description and sample sizes. By description, they meant grounded theory used comparative analysis to generate a theory of processes originating from the data collected. Glaser and Strauss further declared that systematically obtained data made the results of the findings have *predictable* outcomes that are *explainable, interpretable,* and have an *applicable* use (1967). All three are specifically important for marginalized African-Americans, especially the potential to apply theory in opposition to T2DM in the culture. Additionally, they believed researchers could apply the theory to *any* sample size and gave a hospital ward and classrooms in schools as examples. The grounded theory also builds upon Mead and Morris' (1934) and Dewey's belief that action and interaction create knowledge (Corbin & Strauss, 2007). This concept is the same as symbolic interactionism where the basis of a person's action is their interpretation of what they observe within their social constructs, rather than an impulsive reaction.

Although this study incorporated multiple theorists, it extensively followed the latest revision of "Techniques and Procedures for Developing Grounded Theory" (Corbin & Strauss, 2007), surreptitiously relying on their wisdom through the entire process of developing the grounded theory. Other supportive works were from Birks and Mills (2011) means of coding. Also of significant value were Charmaz (2011) diagrams on the grounded theory process and memo writing and Patton's (2002) viewpoints of building theory. Helpful also was Creswell (2007) states that "the intent of grounded theory is to move beyond description and to generate or discover a theory, an abstract analytical schema of a process" (Creswell, 2007, pp. 62–63).

Nevertheless, Corbin and Strauss' (2007) observations guided this study to avoid the mistakes they noted that some researchers made in calling their methodology grounded theory when producing thick descriptions or case studies, and not theory. Therefore, starting with the data collection, this study focused on finding a theory that connected faith, knowledge, and the Afro-Theistic social constructs of African-American COGIC members with T2DM.

The grounded theory began with inductive reasoning; that is, gaining a general understanding of particular cases by finding patterns in the data leading to the development of categories (Birks & Mills, 2011). Abductive reasoning followed the induction by making unconventional connections between the emerging patterns (Birks & Mills, 2011). The theory appeared grounded in the data through constant comparative and theoretical sampling until data saturation, as noted by reoccurring processes (Charmaz, 2011; Corbin & Strauss, 2007). A comparative analysis of the data focused on the details (incidents) of the data and evaluating it for multiple meanings. The coding consisted of primary and secondary coding including axial (memo writing), focused, abstracting, theory building, and, finally, theoretical sampling to answer questions stimulated along the way. Altogether the data revealed concepts with each iteration of incidents, codes, and compared processes within and across interviews (Birks & Mills, 2011; Charmaz, 2011).

The constant comparative methods also included qualitative researchers reading excerpts for feedback from their perspective. The comparisons continued until conceptual categories emerge. At this point, theoretical sampling, which relied heavily on the memo writings of the conceptual categories, identified the type data needed for a particular concept (Charmaz, 2011). Theoretical sampling continued until saturating the abstract categories, which rendered them credible and lucid. Following Birks and Mills's example of using the word "memo" as an acronym helped in the discovery of a core category. MEMO means "Mapping research activities; Extracting meaning from the data; Maintaining momentum; and Opening communication" (2011, p. 40).

Comparative analysis continued with abductive reasoning through each step that moved the study toward the abstract, where a theory emerged grounded in the data. The advanced coding consisted of the development and use of diagrams as recommended by Corbin and Strauss (2007). Theoretical integration followed which resulted in "a comprehensive explanation of a process or scheme apparent in relation to particular phenomena" (Birks & Mills, 2011, p. 12). The symbolic interactionism in this study consists of the African-Americans in the COGIC church combining their Afro-Theistic faith and knowledge of T2DM with their Afro-Theistic social constructs from Chapter 3 and is fundamental to the data analysis.

Part 3
Background and Methodology

Part 3 reveals the researcher's and the participants' background and develops the theoretical framework or model of inquiry that directs the study. Chapter 8 is an expansion of Afro-Theism and reveals the researcher as the emic or insider for this study, who used it as motivation for completing the study. The chapter discusses the emic perspective that sets the precedence for the study. Chapter 9 establishes the Afro-Theistic theoretical framework as an integral part of African-American studies investigated through the data provided by the participants. Finally, it develops the theoretical framework that continues with the researchers' paradigm that includes the importance of symbolic interactionism.

8 Researcher's Perspective

The researcher's perspective is as the emic or insider for this study with the same background as the Church of God in Christ (COGIC) members with type 2 diabetes mellitus (T2DM) chosen as the participants. The nearness of his historical roots supersedes the founding of the COGIC in 1897 (Whitehead, 2001a) since his grandfather and former slave (see Figures 3.2 and 8.1) donated the land for the only COGIC church in East Texas country community. The grandfather's son, the researcher's dad, an ordained elder born in 1888, possibly knew the COGIC founder, Bishop Charles Harris Mason. The researcher's mother was a missionary in this church. Furthermore, in 1995, the researcher was ordained as an elder in this COGIC denomination as well.

In 1979, before the researcher's conversion to Christianity, he became a member of a historically Black fraternity called Phi Beta Sigma, an organization dedicated to serving others, especially within the African-American community. After the ordination, he completed a Master of Ministry and a Doctor of Ministry from Louisiana Baptist University that resulted in doctrinal differences, primarily concerning speaking-in-tongues that differed from his COGIC ordination. Nevertheless, his ordination qualified him to pastor a congregation or establish a COGIC church. After the ordination, he incorporated an interracial Bible Church. Ironically, when he sought advice from his White brother, who was ardently against

Figure 8.1 (a) Sketch and (b) Photo of Henry: Grandfather 1853–August 7, 1930.

speaking-in-tongues, he gave him the cold shoulder when he mentioned having an interracial church. For more than 17 years, his indifference reminded the researcher of the separation that cultural differences cause. Also, and concurrent with his ordination, the researcher received a degree in medical technology (MT), today known as Medical Laboratory Science (MLS). As a nationally certified medical laboratory scientist and with continual education, he accepted an appointment as a professor in the Clinical Laboratory Science department at the Texas State University.

Congruent with his ordination, certification as an MT, and continual education, he is a diabetic patient. His presentation of the research finding in 2016 led to his selection and current position as the Chair of Chemistry and Urinalysis for the American Society for Clinical Laboratory Science (ASCLS), the only professional organization exclusively for medical laboratory scientists. Finally, his spirituality, education, and health converge in the emergence as a qualitative researcher in adult education.

To date, he has conducted quantitative research on the prevalence of prediabetes among college students that are under stress. His interest in prediabetes and diabetes extends from the tragedies above and also having diabetes. Diabetes is also a concern as a citizen since it ranks as the seventh leading cause of death in America and its complications can lead to coronary heart disease (CHD), the leading cause of death in America. His journey as a diabetic patient has crossed many learning educational settings with varying degrees of effectiveness toward long-term changes in health behaviors. For example, the announcement that he had diabetes had an effect that resulted in his severely modifying his diet for more than five years, but then he picked up some of the old dietary habits. His hospitalization resulted in him modifying and monitoring his diet enough to prevent a repeat of that event. Through a literature review of transformative learning of diabetics, in studies such as Davis-Smith (2007) and Bricker et al. (2010), he discovered the existence of support groups for those with diabetes. Consequently, he sought out counsel by diabetes educators and participated in a support group congruent with the recommendations of researchers from literature reviews (Gay, Mills, & Airasian, 2006; Mills, 2007).

For example, his interview with a diabetes educator created a lasting impression of hope that has not dissipated. As a result, he attended several support group meetings for those with diabetes and obtained individual diabetes counseling that has led to a greater awareness of the need for diet control and exercise. At no time did his primary care physician suggested or mentioned the existence of support groups for people living with diabetes. Nevertheless, despite the benefits of the support group and the individual diabetes educational sessions with a diabetes educator, they also revealed some problems.

One of the problems with the support group is a matter of belonging. Although the researcher respected the diabetes educator and those in the group, cultural differences made him an outsider. For example, in one of the meetings, in a joyous moment, the diabetes educator said, "I know; why don't we bring our favorite recipes and share with the group on how we were able to modify them to fit our diabetic diet." Since the researcher was the only African-American present, this left him out because Hispanics' favorite foods were different from his. Furthermore, as a member of the COGIC subculture, questions of reconciling beliefs in living by faith with diabetes education prevailed. In addition to the support group, his insurance policy provided individual sessions with a diabetes educator, but due to its brevity, he did not feel comfortable discussing all on his mind about faith and diabetes.

A theory grounded in the data of the COGIC members combining their faith with diabetes education to construct knowledge that leads to transformation is beneficial to supporters. This understanding frees the leader to dialogue to understand, evaluate, and to identify changes within this subculture of African-American diabetics who believe in living by faith. Subsequently, the discourse provides means of critically reflecting upon what Mezirow (1997) calls "the assumptions upon which our interpretations, beliefs, and habits of mind or points of view are based" (Mezirow, 1997, p. 7). Mezirow also states that transformative learning involves a process: "Once set, we automatically move from one specific activity (mental or behavioral) to another" (Mezirow, 1997, p. 5). Theoretical knowledge of African-American culture should identify essential factors that help facilitate those changes.

Through reflection on the best means of helping diabetic African-Americans, the researcher concluded that he should not ignore the obvious strong subcultural differences within the African-American community and treat all the same. The knowledge that COGIC African-American communities have strong convictions based upon religious differences, with 5.5 million members in America alone was disconcerting. After reflecting, he concluded that the theoretical basis for understanding the subcultural processes of reconciling their faith with diabetes education was the priority. In this way, when developing a support group for African-Americans, a theoretical basis exists for dialogue about subcultural differences. By doing so, this would help prevent marginalization and heightened sensitivity to differences within the African-American community.

9 Theoretical Framework

This study aimed to understand an African-American subculture's way of combining their faith-based practices with their knowledge of diabetes mellitus through a grounded theory methodology, but this approach required a point of reference, theoretical framework, or paradigm. The developed theoretical framework combines the philosophical epistemology of social constructivism from Bandura (1971) and a theoretical perspective or paradigm of symbolic interactionism from Mead and Morris (1934) and Blumer (1969). By systematically examining data, the Afro-Theistic framework made it possible to develop a theory about the COGIC subculture of African-Americans with type 2 diabetes mellitus (T2DM), who except the smaller number of Native Americans and Alaskan Natives combined are the greatest sufferers of diabetes per capita in America (CDC, 2012a; Ennis et al., 2011; Hixson et al., 2011; Norris et al., 2012; Rastogi et al., 2011).

At present, support comes from church-based short-term programs facilitated or supervised by pastors since parishioners trust them for guidance in personal matters. Subcultures hold a significant number of African-Americans who live in the duality of social constructs that influence their beliefs and knowledge that originate from outside those social boundaries. Few studies have attempted to understand the African-American perspective of meaning-making from their familiarity with T2DM, and there was no evidence of this investigation from a subcultural viewpoint, which is essential for knowing what is happening (Glesne, 2011). Inferred by Patton (2002), and already established, the best means of accessing the meaning-making within the context of African-Americans with T2DM in the COGIC church is through a qualitative study. Moreover, as a researcher associated with the COGIC church and an African-American with diabetes, the appropriate theoretical framework or lens used in this study was indispensable. Since this paradigm not only guided the researcher in understanding the participants from their perspective, it is also his.

Theoretical Framework Development

Based on the literature of African-American churches, the Afro-Theistic theoretical framework conceptualizes a filter system that African-American

COGIC diabetic members use in making changes to manage diabetes. This framework suggests that a commonality of faith and powerful social constructs exist in all African-American religious groups. Therefore, the theoretical framework of Afro-Theism is all-inclusive, from those who are passive or fanatical to those who are radical. The use of Afro-Theism refers to African-Americans' worship in assemblies of their local religious persuasions and willfully or passively acknowledges their Afrocentric heritage. The name Afro-Theism merely represents an effort to recognize the existence of all forms of religions that are distinctly African-American without having any group "othered."

Therefore, Afro-Theism acknowledges that Asante's (1988) definition of Afrocentric is valid and originates in Africa. However, he argues from the point of view that connects African-Americans to Africa. Afro-Theism refers to the distinct cultural developments primarily of American slaves influenced by Christianity and other religions in modern times. Afro-Theism includes African-Americans who are not militant and find no reason for relegating Christ as presented in the Holy Bible as the White man's God, especially considering that the book descended from Jews and not Europeans. Furthermore, this is a form of intraracial marginalization known as "internalized racism and color-caste hierarchy" (Turner, 1995). This mentality only causes separation and obscures the fact that the first major Christian growth was Afrocentric and not Eurocentric. Gasque (1995) notes that "around AD 300, Christians formed a majority in parts of the providences of Africa and Asia Minor." Theologians believe that the "eunuch of great authority under Candace queen of the Ethiopians" in Acts 8:27 is the one who introduced Christianity to North Africa.

Furthermore, COGIC members do not fit Asante's motif of Afrocentric and would be othered. However, despite knowing that COGIC interpretation of the Bible is like the European Arminius, their Pentecostal roots are traceable to Montanus AD 172, in Asia Minor. This region had a large following in Africa, which predates Eurocentric influences (Wright, 1995). Montanists preached asceticism, saw visions, often fasted, prophesied, were intensely religious, believed in speaking-in-tongues, and labeled fanatics but not heretics, and excommunicated for unknown reasons, and more (Wright, 1995, p. 87). Wright states, "Through their oracles, they urged Christians to relish persecution: 'Do not hope to die in bed...but as martyrs.' Montanists were 'gloriously martyred' in Gaul and Africa" (p. 87).

Nevertheless, Afro-Theism also infers that African-Americans, who do not subscribe to all of the premises of Afrocentrism, should acknowledge the diaspora and also guard against seeing themselves as European creations or the whip for the White man's religion, which was inferred by Asante (1988). In this vein, theologian Franklin lists Afrocentric as one of the seven spiritual traditions in the Black church (Hayes, 2012).

It seems that the word then applies to African-Americans in general who try to maintain their brand of African heritage. Meaning, they created a style separate from those of European descent, even if the original positions of African heritage are unknown. Parris explains, "slaves nurtured and promoted in various secret assemblies was undoubtedly subversive if, for no other reason than the fact that the slaves were engaged in constructing a means of helping themselves by coopting the religion of the slaveowners [sic]" (Paris, 1995, p. 39).

Noticeably, there are several names throughout this study identifying Americans of African descent, but they reflect the culture of the authors. Hayes noted,

> The change in nomenclature... From Negro to Colored to Black and Afro-American to Black and African-American, and finally to African-American to identify all persons of African descent in the United States regardless of land of origin or time of arrival on these shores.
>
> (2012, p. 186)

This same complexity of religion also exists, as shown by Washington (1964). He said, "The religion of the Negro differs from all others in being defensive, reactionary, and lacking in universal or historical appeal" (Washington, 1964). Asante's efforts to disclose the African identity of the Negro religion is significant and vital to understanding African-Americans and African-Americans understanding themselves. In either case, qualitative studies concerning African-Americans must consider Afro-Theism, as is the theoretical framework of this study.

Paradigm and Symbolic Interactionism

This study reflects a paradigm or theoretical perspective of Afro-Theistic symbolic interactionism (Mead and Morris, 1934; Blumer, 1969) through a logocentric ontology (Derrida, 1976) and constructivist epistemology (Bandura, 1966, 1971, 1977; Davidson & Davidson, 2003). In short, Afro-Theism is the written or spoken word plus the nonverbal symbols or communication of the social group that results in meaning-making or understanding. In other words, this is what the researcher believed that the study must observe; the Afro-Theistic influences to capture the learning that is taking place. This paradigm is reflective of an African-American pastor, a medical laboratory scientist (MLS), and a professor who teaches laboratory sciences, including diabetes, from a quantitative perspective. However, based on current trends, knowledge about T2DM has not produced a significant change in the way African-Americans manage the disease (CDC, 2012a). Therefore, taking a qualitative approach to interviewing individuals with diabetes gives them space and helped in the discovery of how they construct knowledge about the disease from their religious background. Ultimately, knowing how a few apply and construct knowledge will aid others in helping African-Americans make better decisions in preventing or managing diabetes.

Crotty (1998) described Weber's fervent belief that social sciences differ only regarding interpretivism or understanding. Crotty states, "as Weber sees it, both the natural sciences and the human and social sciences may be concerned at any given time with either the nomothetic or the idiographic" (1998, p. 68). Nomothetic refers to natural laws (nomos, Greek), and idiographic refers to individuals (idios, Greek). Applied to this study, it means that African-Americans as individuals, who have diabetes, need more exposure to those offering help in managing the disease. The need exists for exposure through publications, both written and verbal, to help those, including pastors, understand what those with T2DM believe and know, and what actions follow because of this knowledge. In theory, determining the knowledge and its application results from in-depth analysis of interviews when viewed through the symbolic interactions of this African-American COGIC subculture with T2DM.

Symbolic Interactionism

Symbolic interactionism afforded the production of any credible and applicable theory (Corbin & Strauss, 2007). In essence, symbolic interactionism is a way to understand individuals who create knowledge through social constructs. Patton (2002) noted that theorists make a distinction between constructivism and social constructionism, the former being individualistic meaning-making and the latter being the imposing societal forces of meaning that individuals accept as their own. Patton (2002, p. 97) also notes that "It remains to be seen whether this distinction will gain widespread use since the two terms are so difficult to distinguish and easy to confuse..." Without splitting hairs, this study combined the meaning of constructivism by believing that individuals make meaning over time, from pressures and prompts of their long-term social groups. Therefore, the epistemology of this study is constructivism with a logocentrist ontology. This ontology is reflective of Derrida's (Prasad, 2007) logocentrist that stresses the importance of words while acknowledging the contributing factors of social constructs that guide the development of thoughts and actions. Like Derrida's use of the word logocentrist in deconstruction, individuals evaluate and "construct" new meaning through social knowledge and empirical strata or living (Bennett & Bell, 2010).

This qualitative inquiry acknowledges the importance of giving adult learners respect for their knowledge as expressed in Knowles's sixth principle of an adult learner (Hansman & Mott, 2010; Knowles, 1970; M. K. Smith, 2002). The motivation to gather knowledge outside the social constructs of African-Americans with T2DM identifies vital processes of being self-directed learners. These motivating factors provide points for these adult learners to evaluate and question prior assumptions (deconstruction) that lead to the subsequent construction of new meaning. The basis of this development connects to the social constructs of African-Americans subcultures with diabetes that leads to personal interpretation and application, in the vein of Mead (Blumer, 1969; Crotty, 1998; Mead & Morris, 1934). Acting as a redactor of Mead's works, Blumer (1969) identified three premises of Meads' symbolic interactionism:

> That human beings act toward things on the basis of the meanings that the things have for them....that the meaning of such things is derived from, or arises out of, the social interaction that one has with one's fellows....that these meanings are handled in, and modified through, an interpretative process used by the person in dealing with the things he encounters.
>
> (p. 2)

For the African-American COGIC members with diabetes, it means ascertaining two things: (1) the meaning diabetes has for them and (2) actions taken to resolve the problem. Action taken or not taken results from the significance placed on T2DM, which comes from the interpretation (understanding) given by COGIC member's faith, knowledge, and social construct. Knowledge of the participants' symbolic interactionism provides the path to understanding the meanings and actions toward the participants solving problems associated with T2DM. Therefore, an understanding of the participants must begin with the discovery of their symbolic interactionism, as seen in later chapters of Part 4.

This chapter began with an explanation of the researcher's constructivist epistemology, and that expanded into an underlying logocentric ontology and included a detailed look at the theoretical framework guiding this study. This framework establishes Afro-Theism as an essential part of the faith, knowledge, and social constructs of the COGIC participants in this study, whether stated or not. The chapter defends qualitative analysis using interviews as the method and grounded theory as a methodology of understanding this African-American subculture of T2DM sufferers. This study's use of the grounded theory methodology followed other theorists' recommendation to researchers using that methodology.

Part 4
Data Collection and Analysis

Part 4 discusses the data collection and data analysis using the grounded theory methodology and shows its significance in preserving and giving preeminence to the voices of the African-Americans in the COGIC diabetic subculture. Eventually, the permeated learning (PL) theory resulted from the analysis. To make this connection, Chapter 10 begins with the interview of the participants in their community setting. Chapter 11 maps the Afro-Theistic symbolic interactionism of actions, interaction, and emotions grounded in their data needed to understand "what is going on here." Finally, Chapter 12 takes a brief look at data analysis without all the details. Therefore, Part 4 is the key to the construction of new meaning related to type 2 diabetes mellitus (T2DM) and the consequent theory developed through principles of adult learning as discussed in the final parts of the book.

10 Interviews

The thick and rich data of only five individuals provided enough information to meet the goals of this study. That is, through analysis of these data emerged major and minor concepts, categories, and the central category necessary in grounded theory. Furthermore, each category evolved entirely with data saturation from repeated examples, making it unnecessary to interview more individuals. This evidence provided a sufficient understanding of how faith, knowledge, and social constructs worked together for COGIC members with type 2 diabetes mellitus (T2DM). The permeated learning (PL) theory emerged out of thick data like the following excerpts from the participants using a methodology called grounded theory. In the simplest explanation, grounded theory is the use of participants' words to allow a theory to emerge out of concepts discovered by the researcher. Enough of the participants' words are included to comprehend the breadth of data and thoughts flowing naturally from open-ended questions asked of these individuals that are woven seamlessly into the fabric of the permeated learning theory, moving beyond transformative learning, to how these are learning as living beings with mental capacity, do learn.

Arianna

Arianna is a lifelong member of the COGIC denomination. Meaning, she was born to at least one parent with a membership in the church, which is the most common form of this church association. Arianna's encounter with diabetes was typical of others in this study diagnosed with type 2 diabetes mellitus (T2DM). She was an African-American and was in her middle age (the early fifties) when her doctor said she was borderline for T2DM. This discovery came during a routine physical examination with her primary care physician. Arianna received general warnings that she needed to watch her diet. The doctor did not give her a referral to see a dietician but reading material on what she should do about her situation instead. Arianna states, "They might have told me something about the diet. I can't say they didn't give me material, but I didn't read it." Therefore, this "borderline" condition continued in a steady state for more than two years without any change in the stance taken by either Arianna or her doctor. Eventually, based on laboratory results (i.e., hemoglobin A_{1c}) the doctor proclaimed that Arianna had T2DM.

The uniqueness of Arianna's story is her perspective of the diagnosis. The announcement did not faze Arianna in the slightest because she did not believe that she had T2DM. Moreover, she seemed impertinent about the questions asked concerning T2DM. The abrasion did not reflect in the interview since previously and voluntarily, a participant mentioned Arianna's adamant disbelief that a problem existed. With contempt, she kept rapping her fingers making a "pa-thump, pa-thump, pa-thump" sound while probing regarding the initial diagnosis of T2DM as if to say we might as well move on to other questions. This attitude was not a case of denial, since she gave the reason for her stance, saying,

> The numbers say it, but I don't really know if I do [believe it]. I just had to go by what they say because like I say, I don't feel [painful]; I have never had any symptoms of it—that I'm aware of.

The tone of her voice suggested she thought the doctor erroneously forced her to surrender and start taking medicine.

Based on her reply, there were two problems with the diagnosis. First, she did not have any symptoms or evidence to prove that she had diabetes other than laboratory test results. In other words, in Arianna's mind, there is a disconnection between laboratory results and indicated diagnosis without physical evidence. When probing for the reason, she felt that she needed to have physical symptoms before a diagnosis; Arianna revealed that she had many years of experience working with patients with T2DM. Later, Arianna gave more insight for her definition of diabetes as proof that she did not have diabetes. She stated:

> We just had a session at church Tuesday. But far as before then. We have family members, church members, diabetic family members. And I do know people that, you know, have had to take insulin and all this, young, my age or whatever. But I probably should take it more serious than I have, but I guess because last week when I was tested, my blood sugar was okay. I never felt whatever. I do take the pill, although he first started me off with one pill a day and then, I guess the number changed a little, whatever, he changed it to a half in the morning and one at night. Well, I'm just bad about taking medicine. So I really never took that half in the morning, maybe a couple of times. So, I'm still taking the one at night.

In her estimate, a person with diabetes (young or old) takes insulin, or at the least have elevated blood glucose (sugar) results. She believed the home glucose test was the best indicator of her status or at least as good as the hemoglobin A1$_c$ the doctor (according to Arianna) used to confirm his diagnosis. She reasoned that a glucose reading within normal ranges, even with periodic testing, was proof that she did not need medicine (pills) for diabetes, at least not the dosage prescribed by her doctor. Medicine then is the second problem expressed by those interviewed, a general distrust, and fear that the medication caused more harm than good.

Finally, Arianna's belief about her diabetes status presented a conundrum in connecting her faith with diabetes. However, after unraveling the mystery, it provided a valuable link with the comments of other participants. Her responses also helped make a connection between a seemingly indifference to doctors concerning the prevention of diabetes and a later diagnosis of cancer. Regarding the instructions for diabetes prevention, she stated:

> Watch my diet, exercise, blah, blah, blah, blah, but when I work, I walk, they say walking ain't the same, but I walk pretty much of my day. I work 8 hours, and I know I'm working at least 6 or more of them hours, and by the time I get home, I don't even want to go walking.

However, her attitude completely changed toward a diagnosis of cancer, based on laboratory results without symptoms. She stated, "Now, [in] actuality, as far as going to my primary physician, it's been a while since I've seen him because I came up with the issue in…where I had cancer." She completely dismissed the fact that she had T2DM and focused on her cancer that she considered a more pressing matter.

Glenn

Unlike the other participants, Glenn, an African-American male in his mid-fifties, is a relatively new member of the COGIC denomination. Church affiliation means that he recently became a born-again Christian, also known as receiving salvation or the new birth. COGIC associates true members as those professing new birth. Although a person can have their name added to the membership roster, full-fledged membership comes through conversion to Christianity. One of the marquee songs for the church declares:

> This is the church…Of God…In Christ…(Vamped and repeated)… Oh, you can't join in…You got to be born (drawn out) in…this is the church…Of God…In Christ…(Then repeated).

This mindset is noteworthy and significant because new members are usually long-term holdouts to conversion because they understand the church's position that conversion is a sincere and lifetime commitment to obedience to Christ in every phase of life. Before this pledge, holdouts believe the denomination is too restrictive for the lifestyle they desire to live. However, after conversion, a sincere belief (faith) resonates with all that new converts say and do. Glenn reveals his wholeheartedness as he laments his past wayward actions and celebrates his new conversion. Glenn stated, "...but I ain't been too long got in the church myself, and I thank God for it, but I was out there, it was like, in the world, big time, big time, big time, you know."

This subservient attitude of finally willing to listen to others carries over into his attitude toward his diagnosis with T2DM. Glenn displayed an attitude of learning, was unassuming, and willing to obey any instructions, but exposed many gaps from insufficient instructions. Gaps in knowledge are evident from the beginning of the interview. Glenn began:

> Well, I know a little about diabetes. I don't know much. I've just been diagnosed with diabetes, and here in the last year, the doctors was telling me I was at borderline, so here in the last six months he put me on metformin, and he had me to check my, he—gave me some papers to check my diabetes. So, I've been ranging sometime—97, 125, in that area, might go up to 130, then it will go down to 100, like that. I wasn't sure. I assumed it wasn't the normal range for it to be in.

Glenn only received two tidbits of information about diabetes from his doctor: he knew that he was borderline for diabetes for approximately one year, after which he acknowledged his status changed to T2DM. Without questioning the doctor's diagnosis, his communication with Glenn, his patient is abysmal. The doctor made his diagnosis based on lab results without any physical symptoms, without reason, but with instructions to take some medicine and check his glucose without long-term goals or purpose other than keeping his glucose readings low. Glenn did not receive a reason for the onset of diabetes nor how to prevent it while he was borderline. Glenn did not appear overweight, nor did he indicate that the doctors thought he had a problem with obesity. Glenn was aware of the connection between T2DM and obesity as indicated when he said, "...I told them (church members, assumed) it's going to be hard for the Saints to lose some weight because we always eating."

By all indications, the attitude toward Glenn's T2DM was mundane as another person with diabetes and therefore undeserving of viable knowledge. This treatment is evident when he said, "...he—gave me some papers to check my diabetes," and expected Glenn to figure out how to take his glucose reading without a demonstration. Glenn surmised it was the color of his skin and he noted the difference when he said, "...him in the next room, taking his time with people staying in there a long time...he [is] a different color, you know what I'm saying?" Over the years, Glenn had noticed the doctor spent more time with his White clients than with him. Glenn's proof that some White people assumed that because he was Black, he was also ignorant; he decided to test his theory.

Since his doctor did not demonstrate how to use the glucose meter, he took it to a local Walgreens pharmacist. He stated:

> Just like when I got the machine, nobody showed me, so I came home, and I said, it's easy to do once you do it, but had never used it before, you know what I'm saying? So, I got here, and I went back up to the store about eight miles, and I took it in there and said yall show me how to use it, so I can make sure this, and that. They say, "Oh, it's easy [in a mocking voice]…I said, "show me," then when he got it to do it, and he couldn't really do it, right then, himself; you know what I'm saying?

Glenn demonstrated his sincere desire to learn and asked if he could demonstrate what he had learned. Captured in the field notes is this: "During voluntary glucose testing, Glenn did not clean his finger, the fact is, after reading the meter, he sucked the blood to stop the bleeding." Glenn's willingness to learn was not matched by his doctor's willingness to teach, as noted in another field note.

Glenn was searching for answers:

> I gave him as little as possible to prevent me from interfering with the research questions. He absorbed all of my information and used it to improve his knowledge of diabetes mellitus.

Glenn's understandable frustration was the belittling void in instructions to someone willing to fix the problem. Another field note records a major reason to believe Glenn's sincerity.

> He [Glenn] spoke with tears in his eyes… When he said, "I know you know," I am certain he [Glenn] was referring to my uncontrollable tears the day before. My tears were a reference to Jesus being nailed to the cross in a skit [performed by church youths on Sunday at the local COGIC church]. It was emotional because two days prior, we had an awards ceremony for Kathleen Aguero, one of our students in the Clinical Laboratory Science program, who was killed in a car accident over spring break. Plus, I had a brother [who] died a few weeks prior to that, and an Uncle who was a Bishop in the COGIC church who died prior to that. A tough year for me… At Kathleen's ceremony, Dr. Rohde said he could not see how I could hold back the tears. I said, [it] was a sense of duty as a minister. But, just before I spoke as a guest speaker on Sunday following the ceremony, I had a long moment of tears.

Glenn opened his heart helped convey the understanding of the genuineness one may have in learning to manage T2DM, the frustrations one may encounter, and the sense of futility when this void in knowledge remains unfilled. Glenn was one of the attendees at the support session instituted by Jane. From this meeting, the following showed his attentiveness to details and proved his willingness to learn, saying:

> And I know like—you know, you learn more as you go like we had a session at the church the other night and Brother…was talking about it 'cause he's a diabetic, but he said he's not now 'cause he eat the right things and stuff, he's saying.

Glenn, apparently moved by what he learned at the meeting, helped validate the importance of this study and confirm his willingness to fix the problem. He demonstrated more proof of his desire to learn when he changed doctors. After finally changing doctors, he stated:

> But the doctor that I have now…he do set down and talk to me like you talking to me and had to tell him, man, I sure appreciate you telling me that, but you know, the doctor that I had years before that, you know that doctor…I tell you what the doctor I got now stayed in that room with me longer the first time, longer than my other doctor did, three to four years.

Hearing Glenn's story evoked several questions, "What is the doctor's responsibility in educating potential T2DM patients about their condition?" What is the goal of medication? How possible is it for T2DM patients to stop needing diabetes medicine? What does diabetes management mean? Regardless, Glenn's interview added valuable information to this study in knowing how faith, knowledge, and social constructs worked together in the COGIC subculture.

Livia

Livia is a mature lifelong member of the COGIC denomination. Like most participants, her family can trace their membership back to the founder and even the formation of the COGIC church. Livia is a vibrant, mature African-American female who is active within the denomination. She retired from the medical field and served as a sounding board for many within the community concerning spiritual and health issues. Livia conscientiously influences family members and community members with admonitions to maintain a healthy lifestyle. Perhaps this is the reason Livia expressed the most surprise, embarrassment, and frustration after being informed that she had T2DM. Her diagnosis came later in life and a few years after retirement. Livia stated:

> I was diagnosed, which was kind of discouraging, I was diagnosed April of last year, and that's something I said would never happen to

me, and I was diagnosed. I did some routine lab work, and when it came back, my blood sugar I think was like 150, but my hemoglobin A_{1c} was 8 point something, and I'm like, you've got to be kidding me.

Like others in this study, Livia did not exhibit noticeable physical ailment or symptoms of T2DM. Instead, like others, her doctor's decision resulted from laboratory tests. Unlike the other participants, Livia had a greater understanding of the cause of diseases and the significance doctors placed on laboratory tests. For example, she described diabetes in this manner: "Well, I know it's dealing with your pancreas and insulin." Therefore, the previous quote exhibits her understanding that the diagnoses of diabetes come from the combination of laboratory tests. She did not lack knowledge of T2DM and had cared for diabetic patients. For certain, her knowledge of T2DM is the primary source of her frustration.

Livia believes part of the problem is that the test results doctors rely on to make their diagnosis. She stated:

> Well too to me and this is the way I feel, the range back when I started, I started working July 21st, 1980, I was a fresh graduate... and the range that they had for your blood sugars was a lot higher then, than now. They keep lowering the blood sugar levels. So, if they keep lowering the blood sugar levels, everybody in this world going to be a diabetic.

The word "lowering" evoked the thought that the current numbers did not consider ethnic variations of African-Americans, and the authorities could manipulate numbers to include everyone at will. For certain, Glenn would come to this conclusion from a community leader like Livia. Particularly considering that he said, "One time, they did have me thinking just White people couldn't get it, diseases like diabetes and high blood pressure." Furthermore, as a laboratory scientist and African-American with diabetes, her comments were sobering and previously not considered. Coincidentally, her education in the medical field coincided with the researcher as a medical laboratory technician in the U.S. Air Force, which resulted in a promise to search old references to verify her claim. Livia's claim was right; experts lowered the results that indicated T2DM based upon a fasting glucose test from 149 to 129 mg/dL.

As further proof, Livia, as did all participants, made a comparison of their status with a family member, primarily in the form of an ancestor. Livia said of her dad:

> It makes me wonder 'cause like my dad was diagnosed at 70-something years old as a diabetic. There is no way, that was true, and the only reason, the only time my dad's blood sugar went up, and that's how you knew he was sick. When he had his—he had I think it was a

triple bypass or a quadruple—anyway, he had a bypass surgery, and his blood sugar went up, and so they said, of course, he was diabetic, and they were going to put him on medicine, whatever. My dad got out of the hospital; he said God had gave him all the years that he promised. He was going to eat what he wanted, and he did just that. My dad didn't have bad hemoglobin A_{1c}, so what gives with that? And he always was a guy who loved fresh—he liked his peas and his beans and his okra, he loved his bacon, he loved his squash, he loved his grits, he loved his eggs, his fried corn.

Livia used her dad in his old age as an example to prove that the diagnoses of diabetes will happen to anyone because the numbers that indicated T2DM had changed. She claimed her dad did not have diabetes for several reasons. His blood glucose (sugar) became elevated when he had heart problems. In other words, she considered that his elevated glucose served to warn him of his heart condition. In her logic, diabetes would have been evident before his old age. She also noted that in all her dad's laboratory tests, only the less reliable one met the condition for diabetes. She surmised that since the more reliable analysis producing the hemoglobin A_{1c} result was within the reference range for nondiabetic individuals, the doctor made the wrong diagnosis. She used his diet of unprocessed foods as another reason to question the doctor's decision.

Furthermore, her dad did not believe he had diabetes, or at least the diagnosis was not currently relevant. His attitude toward the diagnosis of diabetes gave a clear example of how COGIC members weave faith into their decision-making processes. In her dad's case, he thought God had given him a meaningful life, and he decided to live the remainder of his life in a manner substantive to him without the restrictions of doctors.

However, Livia admitted that obesity was a problem within her COGIC community, and she admitted to having a weight problem. Therefore, she worked hard on weight reduction through diet and exercise, but knee problems that developed thwarted her efforts. Subsequently, Livia believes there should be a quick cure for those testing positive for diabetes with weight being the only physical evidence that a problem exists. For this reason, Livia states:

> 65 pounds and I felt real good about myself and these years went on, and you know, the weight came back up. So, it's just kind of disheartening because everybody say do this and do that and it's not like I don't want to. But if I'm in pain, then to me it's not an option, and I just feel like I should have a quick fix, do you know what I mean?

The prompting to lose weight came from her doctors. Later she echoed their chant, saying, "Well, lose weight, lose weight, I hear that 24/7 and you know, get my eating under control, about eating the right things."

However, one of the things that added to her problems was the socialization during and after events at the church. She said, "Church folks like to eat. We like to eat and especially if you go to a service, like a convention or whatever, I don't care what time of night you get out, you going to eat something." The reason for not curtailing the eating when a problem exists extends from the fact that it did not immediately worsen the effects of T2DM. She continues, "because we feel good or whatever, we just keep doing what we're doing, we just keep eating and keep eating the sweets and keep eating because we don't feel anything." Celebratory eating is a common and predictable attitude, considering the ethnic background related to the uncertainty of life. In other words, prejudice and poverty threatened their parents and their early childhood in the South. As a result, they celebrated with the immediate gratification of community feasts, and it has become a way of living.

Carlos

Carlos is a middle-aged African-American male with a lifelong membership in the COGIC denomination. His family also traces their heritage back to the church founder and the formation of the COGIC church. He and his family are active church leaders locally, within their state, and nationally. Carlos's diagnoses of T2DM came after many years of warning. When he was younger, the doctors informed him that based upon his family history, he was a good candidate for T2DM. Carlos stated:

> Well, with me, my doctor, every year I take a physical. I've been doing that since...I kept that going and then the jobs I've had somewhat demanded that you take a physical, so I've always done that. And every year, the doctor would ask me about my family, and I would answer questionnaires, what have you and when I let them know that my two brothers at that time had it and pretty much, the doctor would always tell me, at some point, you probably going to contract it as well.

Carlos continued:

> So, that would always be in the back of my mind, but at the time, I was kind of young. You know, I was kind of young, so I'm like, yeah, sure, you know. He would always say; you're alright, watch it a little bit, though that number is up a little bit high, but you're fine. So, every year I went like that.

Each year it seemed that Carlos inched closer to the predicted status of T2DM. It seemed that regardless of the warnings to watch his weight and maintain a healthy diet, Carlos drifted toward self-fulfilled prophecy. Not until later did Carlos revealed that feeling, saying, "So he wasn't a cheerleader, pretty much prophesied that one day, of course, he was right." Carlos needed help but received negative predictions instead.

Those in the COGIC denomination are people of faith and sensitive to predictions, which they consciously or unconsciously translate into prophecy from trustworthy individuals. Carlos's revealing statement "always be in the back of my mind" is significant. Although COGIC members are not ignorant or naïve, they have a high capacity to tolerate those in authority. Often quoted is the biblical passage that says, "Touch not my anointed and do not my prophet any harm." Furthermore, from the church's origin, those proclaiming to be working on behalf of God has precedence over educational status. Carlos reveals this reverence of doctors concerning diabetes by saying:

> Faith is one thing, but God, you know, he made doctors for a reason. We're made in the image of God. God is creative and so; a part of God is in us and so, I mean, look at man. Look at all the great things man has done.

Notably, Carlos contrasts his faith with the doctors' diagnosis. Therefore, in his estimate, doctors command the same respect as church authorities, each being part of God's creation.

Earlier, Carlos mentioned another significant factor that affects his decisions following the general warning about the possibility of T2DM—"youth." Youth was also a factor with Nick, the final participant, which connects him to Carlos. However, in Carlos's case, youth led to a cursory acknowledgment of the possibility without action. Therefore, a general warning left room for Carlos to interpret or decide on the best course of action that invariably resulted in only slight dietary modifications. Atypically, Carlos did not like sweets; his ancestral heritage was the desire for meat and potatoes instead. Affirmingly, he states,

> Well, sweets and stuff never bothered me, but when you start talking about starches and potatoes, you know, I grew up on that, so I give up your drink as a habit, but I can't give up potatoes. I grew up with that stuff, so.

Like every participant except Arianna, Carlos admitted that the weight was a contributing factor to T2DM. Moreover, he admitted that his continual weight gain mirrored the advancement of his condition toward T2DM.

Carlos's mantra concerning T2DM is "FEAR." Not until the doctor mentioned that he had diabetes did his attitude change from inactivity to fixing the problem. The initiating factor was fear as he stated:

> My doctor's encouraged me. He tell me I got diabetes that's encouragement. That's what motivates me, the fear of having diabetes

motivates me. People are different; they may need a coach, somebody to motivate them, but I don't need it. I need, the fear. I'm a Pentecostal boy. I initially got saved because of fire insurance.

During the interview, Carlos reveals the source of fear evoked within him was when the doctor announced that he had T2DM. He reflected upon ancestors who died of T2DM. Carlos reflected upon the Pentecostal origins of the COGIC denomination style of preaching during his childhood rearing. Outsiders call these "fire and brimstone" messages. COGIC preachers are notorious for preaching that one must come to a believing faith in Jesus Christ, or they will spend eternity in hell where there are only fire and brimstone that produces weeping and gnashing of teeth. This message was to everyone; children included. Even today, COGIC does not believe in "children's church," where the message is toned down. These words produce powerful incentives for youth to live a righteous life and avoid all the trappings that could lead to death.

Therefore, children understand there are only one of two choices, right or wrong. Right; may be called the "do not's." Do not curse, lie, steal, cheat, dance, go to clubs, smoke cigarettes, drink alcohol, commit immoral acts, and, God forbid, overt sins, such as rape and murder. Wrong is just the opposite. As a result, these are common characteristic beliefs of any COGIC member. Ironically, this preaching has the same effect as Orthodox Muslims preaching has on its youth. However, notice Carlos said he "initially" converted to Christianity because of "fire insurance." Although the fear drove him to obedience, biblical scholarship keeps him obedient. Therefore, Carlos's so-called fear factor motivated him to change his health habits and eliminate the threats of T2DM, and listed the loss of limbs, eyesight, and kidney failure as the factors.

However, earlier Carlos also identified another type of fear, that is, the lack of diabetes education. Carlos states:

So our pastor has allowed since we have healthcare professionals here in the church. And as a matter of fact, his daughter is one, and so he's allowed different ones to come in and kind of, educate the people, and that's all it is, is we need education because where there is a lack of education, there's going to be fear.

In other words, he believed that through education, one could avoid another type of fear, that is; fear that comes through ignorance. At the same time, and without stating it here, as he had previously inferred, he was saying there is a healthy fear, one that could motivate those threatened with T2DM into preventive or better management of the disease. He also identifies another authority figure prominent in the diabetes education and management formula. That is, those in leadership positions, especially pastors, whom parishioners look to for guidance. Unfortunately, it took the death of the pastor's wife for him to start addressing the health issues of other church members. Fortunately, through his wisdom and care for the members, he allows the church to have one health awareness session per month to address the health issues of the members.

Nick

Nick is also a middle-aged African-American male with a lifelong membership in the COGIC denomination. Like others, his family also traces their heritage back to the church founder and the formation of the COGIC church. Nick is a zealous and talented church member and renowned local leader. However, Nick's story is the most different of all participants. Unlike others, his development of T2DM came at the relatively early age of 37 years. Unlike the other participants, Nick developed preconditions that forced him to seek medical help.

Ironically, on-the-job benefits may have triggered the onset of diabetes.

For example, he stated, "I would go to the at the 7-Eleven we could drink all drinks for free." Over time, as Nick said, "I started experiencing some things going on with me, I felt wasn't right. I was urinating a lot at night." As a result, he attempted to quench his thirst by drinking his favorite orange flavored Slurpee's, which created a vicious cycle of drinking and urinating. Finally, he said:

> Excessively thirsty throughout the day. And very, after sleeping at night, waking up several times to urinate. While I was at work, I was finding myself falling asleep. Couldn't stay awake. That went on for some time, and I knew something was going on with me. I went to the doctor and told me I was a diabetic, and my blood sugar was like 500.

Excessive thirst and urination are classic symptoms of the two types of diabetes: diabetes insipidus, and diabetes mellitus (see Chapter 4). Excessive sleepiness is also another common symptom of T2DM. The 500 mg/dL glucose reading is dangerously close to resulting in a coma. Before seeking help from his doctor, Nick stated:

> I would drink one and a couple hours later I was so thirsty again, go back and drink another one. I was like I can't stay awake. Sometimes I have to go park somewhere I know no ones at just to try to take a nap. Try to wake up and pretty much the same thing again. Then in church, I started noticing when I really, man this is wrong, something wrong. I would see people's silhouette, but I couldn't see their mouth moving or their eyes, it affected my vision.

The final straw seems to have been his blurred vision while at the COGIC church that finally sent him to the hospital. Eye problems are also classic symptoms of T2DM, which could result from stress, as with the researcher's mother or elevated glucose (sugar), as with Nick. As a result, Nick's doctor insisted that she give him an insulin shot to bring down the glucose reading.

Interestingly and significantly, despite all the symptoms, Nick delayed going to the doctor because he compared his condition to his dad. He stated:

> Yes, and that's what made me really go to the doctor. I thought I could tolerate the peeing and sleeping, but after it got to where I couldn't see, I had to have a doctor check on me 'cause some symptoms I didn't experience. My dad was a Type-2 Diabetic. And I remember—use to say he smelled fruit, and I had never—I don't smell that. And I got afraid when I couldn't see far. They brought it down. They put me on Glucophage.

Like with Carlos, fear was the determining factor that overrode all of Nick's inhibitions to seeing his doctor. Only, Nick lived in denial, but he based his decision on his knowledge about diabetes, which he suspected, but did not have what he deemed as the essential symptoms experienced by his dad with T2DM. The fruity smell of urine is another classic experience by those with uncontrolled diabetes.

This fruity smell is the smell of ketones that results from the body utilizing lipids or fat as an energy source. All body cells, especially the brain, need glucose (sugar) for energy. If cells in the human body do not receive the energy needed to function, as in the case of T2DM, the body will convert fat into glucose. This conversion will result in the production of ketones as a metabolic by-product and disposed of through urination. Incidentally, patients with T2DM, like Nick, have enough glucose, they do not have the insulin that instructs the cells to open and let the glucose enter. The cell does not know it, so the nervous system thinks it is starving and utilize the fat that is available to produce the sugar it must have. However, the increased ketones can lead to the body becoming too acidic, called acidosis, which can also kill those with T2DM.

Unlike Carlos, fear did not force Nick to take the necessary steps to manage T2DM properly. Other obstacles arose as seen in the following statement:

> Which, is known as metformin ~ also. When I first ~ taking that, it got sick to my stomach; I got sick to my stomach. But uh, I got passed it, but I still eat…I didn't still cut out things I shouldn't eat. It controlled it for a period of time. Then I got worse 'cause I feel like I'm invincible, I can live with this stuff. It ain't affecting me like that. So I continued to eat some things I knew I shouldn't have been.

Nick is not living in denial as with Carlos, who lived in imminent danger of T2DM, Nick's youth seems to make him feel he could manage T2DM with a pill along. At some point, he admitted that he made his decisions based upon his desire for sweets. Notably, Nick only mentioned one problem with T2DM medicine, but later he like the other participants express other reasons to avoid taking it. It took two years (age 39) before Nick finally had enough of the medication.

Therefore, it took both time and youth to create a desire to eliminate T2DM and not merely manage it. Nick began by mastering to balance dieting, exercising, and living with the disease. However, this mastering took place in stages over time. He began by exercising. When asked how he knew to do calisthenics, he based it upon common knowledge that exercise is what we need but admitted his that doctor tried to teach him. He said, "She tried to teach me, but you know being young like I was, it was really going in one ear, out the other." His doctor was an African-American who also sent him to a dietician, but Nick was determined to do things his way. By his admittance, the doctor did all the right things, but he attributed the problem to him being, "Young and felt like I could do what I want." However, at some point, Nick grew weary of taking the medication and decided he would stop taking it. He did so by finally modifying his diet to exclude sugar.

Over time, by eliminating the sugar, exercising, monitoring his glucose readings, and without taking the medication, things were good for three years. His diet came from one recommended by his brother of eating certain foods (nonsweets) six times a day. It worked so well that his glucose was consistently average; he then reduced checking to once per month, and finally, he stopped monitoring his glucose altogether. However, after three years, he reverted to his old habits of eating sweets, and the symptoms of diabetes returned.

Nick had a new job and his new doctor, a White male, put him back on Glucophage and added a medicine called Actos. Nick knew the doctor from an injury the doctor repaired some years ago. He had chosen this doctor while in a hospital, he heard the doctor's name mentioned several times over the intercom and decided he must be a good doctor because of his popularity. Nevertheless, at this appointment, this doctor became alarmed at the weight gain, so he put him back on the medicine. Nick researched the medication via the Internet. He discovered the new medication Actos would cause weight gain and stopped taking it. As a result, he lost weight. The doctor decided to try some natural means of controlling diabetes, which he suggested to Nick. The doctor also mentions that Nick had developed high cholesterol, which alarmed Nick more than his physician. Nick had learned to educate himself about his health. Therefore, he said:

> Red yeast rice, something natural you can take that should help you lower it. So, I started taking that, but when I walked out of his office,

> I was like; cholesterol! I didn't know much about it but sounds like I'd been eating too much ~ fatty foods.

Nick had learned to counter negative laboratory results by doing the thing that would make those reports positive. Nick said later, "So I decided well I am gonna do something different. I'm going to cut out beef and pork and stick with chicken, fish, and turkey." As a result, Nick again stated:

> So that was nine years ago this past March. So, I quit eating beef and pork. I went back three months later, and I had also stopped taking the red yeast rice he put me on. And I went back to him three months later to do blood work, and he looked at me and said what're you doing? I said, what're you talking about? He said if I ~ would ask 100 people their cholesterol levels, I would doubt one would be better than yours.

Although Nick became self-educated into controlling his cholesterol levels, he did not control his sugar intake through the same educational means. Sadly, Nick completely relapsed into the same detrimental habits of increased sugar intake, not monitoring glucose levels, which resulted in worse medical conditions than before. Now, middle-aged, Nick had the same excuse as he did when he was younger; that is, Nick thought he was invincible. As a result, his friendly doctor gave him more medication, for a total of three, and one being insulin. This doctor retired, and the White female doctor that replaced him looked at Nick's results and said:

> Oh my god! She said you're a candidate for a heart attack or stroke. The A_{1c} is 13. And she looked at me, she said, you gotta do insulin. I want you to make an appointment with an endocrinologist.

It took these frightening statements to get Nick's attention and him reflecting on his dad dying at the age of 63 from diabetes complication. He said:

> My oldest brother is on insulin, and he's about four years and a couple months older than me. And I'm looking like my older brother's health is worse as my ~ dad's ~ was when he was his age.

Finally, fear drove Nick to change his dietary habits from eating sweets. He also states:

> I was like I'm going to change my diet. When I go there [to the endocrinologist], these numbers are going to change. So, I went to the organics section looking at some things I can start eating, and there

was a White lady that was there, and she picked up, she said, "have you ever tried this stuff?" I said, what is it? She said agave nectar. I said no, what is it for? She said I substitute it for sugar.

Nick purportedly utilized this sugar substitute and ate what he researched and found to be friendly fruit, and the doctor recommended complex carbs. With these changes, Nick finally saw the anticipated results and reduced the medications and said:

So, I started eating oatmeal with blueberries, friendly fruit, adding it in there. I would put a tablespoon of this and make it a little sweeter. So, my next appointment with her was in April. I went to see her in April, and she did blood work and got it back, and she almost jumped out of her chair. I'm so happy for you. You lost 27 pounds, and your A_{1c} is 6.

That was Nick's status at the time, while he served as a mentor in the community and especially to his family. Nick also suffered from a crippling bone-to-bone contact problem with his knees that prevented him from exercises, so his control of diabetes was strictly dietary. He continued to search for remedies to alleviate the pain in his knees but manages T2DM despite this problem through a regimented diet.

From these five participants, it is obvious that learning concerning diabetes is occurring, and changes are resulting, but unlike transformative learning, the participants' means of understanding, learning, if one will, is convoluted, and true change is questionable, at best. These individuals are wrestling with insidious life forces—foreign—and unrelentingly life-threating to an oppressed people struggling to live with diabetes, and in many ways, threats of second-class citizenship. An understanding of the learning begins with an understanding of the complexity of being an African-American and that with their beliefs concerning the existence of a deity.

In summary, following each interview, came a barrage of synchronized events. There was a hastily return to quarters to go over the field notes and fill in observations impossible to know from an audio recording and easily forgotten or confused between interviews. Next came the electronic sending of the recording to a hired translator with the prearranged agreement to return the transcript within hours for the initial memo writings. From either the audio or the transcript, if transcribed in time, came the adjustments, addition, and adaptive approaches to the interview and the questions. Many of the adaptations concerned issues that helped understand the discovered symbols discussed in the next chapter.

11 Search for Symbols

Mapping the Afro-Theistic Symbolic Interactionism

The first step in understanding the participants required knowledge of what impressed them concerning type 2 diabetes mellitus (T2DM). Therefore, the Afro-Theistic symbolic interactionism is the paradigm that identifies the context or circumstances that are the progenitors of the processes (actions, interactions, and emotions) experienced by the Church of God in Christ (COGIC) participants. More simply stated, finding what influenced (symbols) their decisions and understanding in social gatherings concerning T2DM was the first step in developing a theory. The paradigm is the participant's perceptions as they combined their faith, knowledge, and social constructs concerning T2DM. Therefore, the Afro-Theistic symbolic interactionism required an understanding of two entities: first, the context, which defines their environment, and second, the resulting processes, from which they made their decisions.

An initial investigation of the first participant transcribed interview revealed that the context, as seen in Figure 11.1, is the perceptions involved in the decision-making processes. In other words, the environment with the most influence was not external but internalized. The context of perceptions was confirmed and fully developed with subsequent interviews. Whereas they internalized the context as perceptions, the perceptions were of real conditions or associations of those with T2DM, with resultant processes manifested as actions, interactions, and emotions fully delineated in Chapter 13, from which emerged the all-important categories.

The context led to the processes within the African-American COGIC subculture of diabetic participants that were chaotic and demarked with decisions ultimately resulting in living or dying. The processes were psychosocial (Dewey, 1982) in nature and related to their promotion or distraction from healthy living with T2DM. The psychosocial nature of these individuals finds its application in the two aspects of the word. That is, the participants' actions revealed psychological meaning-making with substantial influences from their social constructs. Figure 11.1

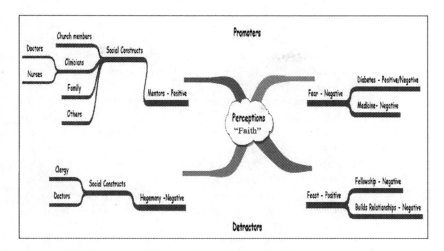

Figure 11.1 Afro-Theistic Symbolic Interactionism—Context and Process.

reveals the left-to-right and top-to-bottom symmetry of the context and processes of the COGIC members' symbolic interactionism. In the following two paragraphs, these dichotomies with an overarching duality of "promoters" and "distractors" are explained.

Promoters of Health

Mentors and fear occupy the upper half of Figure 11.1, which made a significant impact in promoting healthy living of those interviewed. However, these perceptions are in opposition to each other with the left and right symmetry. On the left, mentors are the perceived positive social constructs of the COGIC participants. Their makeup is varied and complex; sometimes individuals or those with equal social status double as detractors. Nevertheless, when identifiable as mentors, the participants perceived them as having a positive influence in their lives.

On the upper right half of Figure 11.1, the participants faced situations that evoked fear, with a negative connotation; participants had mixed perceptions, although overall, the outcomes were positive. For example, when diagnosed with diabetes, the perceptions ranged from disbelief to motivation to fix the problem. In between was those left frustrated and doubtful. Nevertheless, fear provided the greatest motivation in promoting healthy living. Prescription medicine was also necessary for maintaining the health of the participants, but their knowledge-based perception of them was always negative. Therefore, the participants reluctantly took the medication when other solutions would not remediate the adverse effects of T2DM.

78 Data Collection and Analysis

Distractors of Health

The distractors from managing T2DM occupies the lower half of Figure 11.1, which also have left and right symmetry. To the left are the major distractions felt by the T2DM participants, which are the hegemonic social relationships. These social constructs necessitated by religious needs or medical needs distracted from problem-solving through two agents. Clergy, who dictate the social nature of church events that dominates the social lives of faithful COGIC members by ignorance or will, distracts from T2DM members' health through omission. The pastor of the participants corrected this oversight when he became aware of the need to include church service time to address health issues, following his wife's contraction of T2DM. Doctors, on the other hand, marginalized the T2DM participants by failing to let them know what he or she believes is happening. Doctors by will or negligence kept T2DM participants ignorant by issuing medicine without divulging enough information on the drug effects, alternatives, duration, goals, or knowledge concerning the elimination of medication or T2DM.

The lower right half of the distractors are the most difficult branch to manage because the social concept of feasting provides a positive image. However, the physiological results are punitive for those with T2DM. Explicitly stated were the meals following church meetings in celebration or fellowship. Implicit was the strengthening of relationships over shared meals. Nevertheless, the participants admitted that the meals were unhealthy, especially for those with T2DM. As a result, high-calorie foods put the participants in a tug-of-war between relationships and healthy living. The Afro-Theistic theoretical framework provided the paradigm for understanding the participants' symbolic interactionism and highlights the importance of this study as one of qualitative research using grounded theory.

Finally, the center of Figure 11.1 is labeled "Perceptions." Perceptions are the nucleus of the participants' "Symbolic Interaction," or their meaning-making. Perceptions equate to beliefs, later equated to faith, that completes the circle back to Afro-Theism. This observation came late, in fact, years following the study. The significance is that faith became the central category, later developed in terms of the greatest number of codes and the only category connected to the others without inference. Therefore, the later developed category of faith embodies, the participants symbolic interaction, perceptions, and Afro-Theism in relationship to T2DM.

12 Data Analysis

The most crucial part of the data analysis came through trusting the processes of conducting a grounded theory study. As an emerging researcher, spending months analyzing the data without one line written toward the findings required tremendous confidence in Corbin and Strauss's (2007) techniques and processes for developing the grounded theory. The motivation to continue following their advice came from seeing the project unfold toward theory as the participants spoke through coding, memo writing, and making diagrams, just as the authors predicted. The data analysis comes from the theoretical framework of Afro-Theism. It investigated the symbolic interaction of the Church of God in Christ (COGIC) participants with type 2 diabetes mellitus (T2DM) in relation to Afro-Theistic faith, knowledge of diabetes, and the Afro-Theistic construct. Therefore, faith, knowledge, and social constructs assume Afro-Theism, even without explicitly stating it. The open interview questions assisted in generating a credible and trustworthy grounded theory since they resulted in the participants' empowerment to have their experiences with T2DM presented. The theory produced directly applies to the COGIC subculture of African-Americans with diabetes. Overall, the designed analysis revealed the actions, interactions, and emotions related to the participants' faith and knowledge of diabetes through their Afro-Theistic constructs.

The development of a theory grounded in the participants' data that capture their actions, interactions, and the emotions of this subculture demanded trust in the process. Therefore, theory development made it necessary to complete a careful analysis using field notes, many diagrams, and many memos to discover the most salient concepts from the small number of participants. Without the use of diagrams, it would have been impossible to identify the central category that is the basis of grounded theory and to know how to integrate the major and minor concepts that emerged (Corbin & Strauss, 2007). Data analysis would have been impossible without technology such as, MAXQDA 11, which was used to identify, sort, and manage almost 1,600 codes. The utilization of this program illuminated statistical relationships and helped synchronize

80 *Data Collection and Analysis*

the memos and audios with the transcribed data, thus lessening the labor-intensive processes of data management. Another valuable technology used in conjunction with MAXQDA 11 was Inspiration 9, primarily used to draw diagrams or matrices, which represented actions, interactions, and emotions, with refinements that eventually became concepts in many cases. Finally, Inspiration 9 facilitated other memo writings that aided in understanding "what is going on here." The next two sections separately discuss the process of coding, memo writing, and diagramming, but in reality, they were interactively created and grew into an abstraction.

Field Notes

In the process of developing the grounded theory, field notes provided context for the participants' data. For example, Figure 12.1 records the observation of Carlos, a church elder who appeared nervous as seen in the trembling of his left thumb. This observation showed that he questioned whether he was doing the right thing by interviewing for this study. It reemphasized the importance of developing a theory grounded in the participant's data alone. It also revealed his trust that his information served to help COGIC members with diabetes without hurting the church's reputation. Each meeting with a participant included field notes to record observations of the participants' expressions, reactions, moods, emotions, surroundings, and more, related to T2DM.

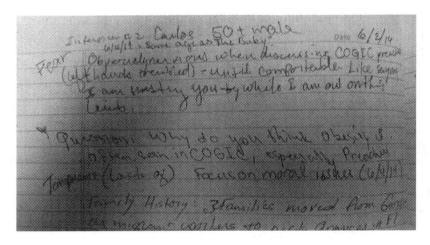

Figure 12.1 Field Notes.

Coding

Coding involved interacting with data (analysis) using techniques such as asking questions about the data, making comparisons between data, and similar. In so doing, concepts emerge to stand for those data, followed by the development of those concepts in terms of their properties and dimensions (Corbin & Strauss, 2007, p. 65).

Following the interview and observational field notes usually came an overnight transcription of the data. Once transcribed, data entry into the MAXQDA (see Figure 12.2) program for storage, coding, and memo writing or axial coding followed as described by Corbin and Strauss (2007).

The purchase and use of the MAXQDA program made it easier to follow Corbin and Strauss (2007), who used the same program to demonstrate the development of grounded theory. The MAXQDA software allowed the storage of data, including, coding, a compilation of all the transcriptions, observational field notes, and audio recordings. The software helped organize and catalog the initial and secondary codes of the participants' data that aided in the development of categories and subcategories. The easily retrievable and viewable database allowed for

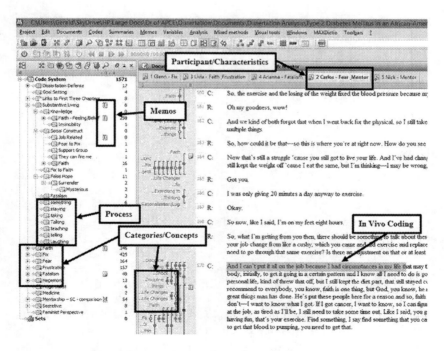

Figure 12.2 MAXQDA—Coding and Memos.

82 Data Collection and Analysis

constant comparative analysis between incidences, codes, and categories, and that led to the abstraction of the participants' data. Reoccurring processes, in vivo codes, and concepts evolved into greater abstractions resulted in the emergence of the definitive categories.

Memo Writing

Memo writing followed each transcription to capture the impression of what seemed to be transpiring in relationship to diabetes in the COGIC subculture. Additional memos in many paragraphs called axial or intermediate coding (Corbin & Strauss, 2007) helped weave primary and secondary codes together in the process of developing categories and subcategories. Later memos reflected thoughts when reading the transcriptions that further helped identify codes, concepts, and eventually processes. In the MAXQDA program (see Figure 12.2), these memos are behind folders with and without letters stamped on them. Those with letters on them came from a constant comparative analysis that focused on incidences leading to abstractions of the data, which assisted in building a theory grounded in the participants' data. The overarching characteristic of each of the participants' tab aided in the comparative assessment of the data at a glance. Evolving diagrams such as those seen in Figure 12.3 inspired new memo writing such as those in the same figure and handwritten memos (not shown). Eventually handwritten memos were incorporated into the MAXQDA program. These memos helped to map and track the theoretical sampling of the participants' data. They continued the abstraction of the data and the development of a theory grounded in the participants' data.

Diagrams

Diagrams can be valuable tools for integration because integrative diagrams are abstract but visual representations of data (Corbin & Strauss, 2007, p. 107). The visualization of the symbolic interactionism (see Figure 11.1) came through iterations of diagrams and memos developed in an Inspiration 9 program (see Figure 12.3). Diagrams in the program aided in identifying concepts, the processes, and their relationships with each other. This mandated time to reflect upon field notes, observations, and thoughts from each interview through memo writing. However, this process took months of interaction between data and drawings. The drawings began as a simple representation of the data but grew in abstraction. Some of the diagrams resulted in dead ends because they did not represent all the participants. Some drawings merged while others grew into concepts and processes. Eventually, a grounded theory emerged through continual comparative analysis, the use of diagrams, and the participants' meaning-making processes involving the

Data Analysis 83

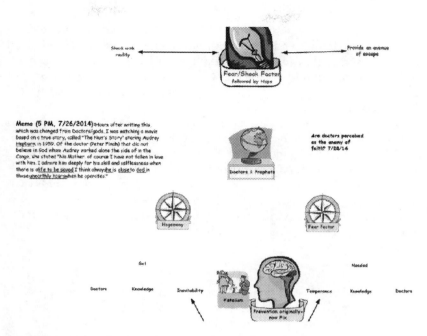

Figure 12.3 Inspiration 9—Memos and Early Diagrams.

participants' COGIC social constructs. Drawings made the abstractions to find an overarching category that connected to all subcategories less daunting of a task, with none greater than Figure 15.1, which resulted in an even greater conceptualization seen in Figure 16.

Credibility and Trustworthiness

The credibility and trustworthiness of the data collected and analyzed came primarily from establishing and maintaining rapport with the participants and their community, similar to Vella (2002). Shared between the researcher and the participants were their historical, ethnic, and church backgrounds, in addition to having T2DM. As a result, participants willingly and passionately spoke concerning their encounters with the disease, which is remarkable for this close-knit community of Pentecostal believers. Their openness to this study extended from trust gained through time spent in the community speaking to its citizens throughout several visits and having a speaking engagement at the COGIC church before the interviews. The participants sensed the genuine love shown to the community and gave invitations to consider their church and community home. Therefore, the trustworthiness of the study is in the open, and detailed data collection and the subsequent systematic analysis through prescribed means of conducting the grounded theory.

84 Data Collection and Analysis

Corbin and Strauss (2007) added that credibility or believability comes from detailed descriptions and the manner of gathering data. Therefore, credibility and trustworthiness merged in the data collection and preanalysis steps involved in triangulating the data. Data triangulation came through the multiplicity of sources. The primary source of triangulation came through the written transcription and hearing the digital recording of the five interviews.

Field notes recorded relevant observations of each participant and their surroundings during the interview, which complimented the digital recording. The triangulated data continued by having a cross section of interviewees, from church leaders to lay members and professionals to laborers and memo writing. Finally, the data contained enough variances in the cases (Charmaz, 2011) to increase the credibility of how faith, knowledge, and Afro-Theistic constructs converged in the COGIC subculture of African-American diabetic members.

Summary

The data collection and analysis resulted from a systematic approach as a necessary component for developing a theory grounded in the data from the participants, with a resulting theory generated purposed to increase support in African-Americans managing T2DM as the motivator. Computer programs like MAXQDA and Inspiration 9 aided in identifying concepts and processes of the COGIC participants with T2DM. Continual comparative analysis of the data and five additional factors (field notes, coding, memos, diagrams, and recordings) helped facilitate the democratic process Knowles et al. (2011) considered vital in hearing the voices of those in this qualitative study. Pseudonyms were selected to obscure any data that threatened the participants' confidentiality and helped facilitate openness during the interviews. Securing the data came through a password-protected computer or placement in a locked file cabinet. Finally, rapport with the participants explains their open discussions, and systematic analysis of the data assured credible and trustworthy results.

Part 5
Emerging Theory

Part 5 is about the actions, interactions, and emotions found the categories that emerged from the participants' data, from which came the permeated learning theory. Beginning with Chapter 13, which discusses the first and most revered category of "fear," and its effects on the participants. Chapter 14 discusses four other categories that emerged from the collected data. From a systematic analysis of these five participants' transcripts emerged the categories discussed in Chapter 15, which gives the anatomy of the core category of "substantive living" from its skeletal parts of five categories and how they connect through actions, interactions, and emotions. Then the chapter, in the same fashion of discovery, names the all-important core category. Although the chapter is long, the details are interesting observations and conversations used to discover the categories and believed necessary for the reader to see the findings as they emerge from the participants. Finally, Chapter 16 reveals how the core category of "substantive living" connects to the five categories by being their motive for existence.

13 Emergent Categories
Fear and Ancestral Mentors

In the next two chapters, the presentation of the categories is made as they emerged and expanded upon the symbolic interactions (Figure 11.1) that introduced the contexts (environment) as the progenitors of chaotic processes. In so doing, concepts emerge replete with examples given by the most salient actions, interactions, and emotions of the participants regarding type 2 diabetes mellitus (T2DM). Some of these examples appeared with the introduction of those interviewed in Chapter 10. More of these examples appear throughout the remainder of this chapter, and still more in the chapter that follows.

Symbolic interactionism identified the context leading to the chaotic nature of processes of the African-American COGIC participants with T2DM whose knowledge-based decisions were matters of living and dying. However, in the chaos, five categories emerge that captures the results of these actions, interactions, and emotions. On the one hand, this chapter developed only one and the next chapter four of the five categories, with the fifth mentioned as the search followed the natural nonlinear chaotic course of discovery with discussions of bias toward living or dying. On the other hand, these five categories tend not to be stable and tumble or ascend into another category with a certain degree of predictability based upon further action, interactions, and emotions that extend from circumstances, events, or situations that first landed the participants into a category. Based on the interviews, the processes of living and dying are psychosocial (Dewey, 1982) in nature, and they linked to the participants' faith, knowledge, and social constructs.

Category 1: Fear

Fear emerged as the dominant category that provokes action toward resolving the myriad of problems with T2DM in COGIC members. However, fear does not always result in positive actions or any action at all. Nevertheless, fear is a major factor that is diverse and complex. Therefore, it necessitated several diagrams to evaluate its impact on the axis of living and dying.

Fear as a Catalyst

In one scenario, fear acts as a catalyst resulting in one of the two reactions depending on the context leading to the participants' perception or interpretation, as seen in Figure 13.1. Initially, some participants were not concerned over the news of T2DM because of desensitizing personal struggles or conditioning of historical problems that anesthetize them to the danger at hand. For example, in one transcribed paragraph, Carlos states, "It seems like we don't get serious about something until they tell you, you could die from it or something." His conclusion about COGIC members reflects both the church's heritage and the ethnic plight of African-Americans living in the South. Chapters 2, 3, and 4 discuss the history of both and explain the necessity of a greater fear to disorient the catatonic response to lesser threats, including T2DM. In other words, the participants can only respond to a limited number of problems, and only immediate threats to living from the adverse effects of T2DM motivates to change. This lack of motivation is the frustration Livia expressed of her husband at one point captured in the transcription of her interview. She said, "my husband just, he won't take his blood sugar, and his blood sugar will be 300…it just irks me when it gets too high. Then he'll take it."

Moreover, participants revealed that current struggles with problems have the same anesthetizing effects on the response from those with T2DM in the COGIC church. For example, Arianna states, "Now, actuality, as far as going to my primary physician, it's been a while since I've seen him because I came up with the issue…where I had cancer." Overwhelmed, Arianna focused on her most immediate concern with cancer and disregarded T2DM altogether. Other participants, to a lesser

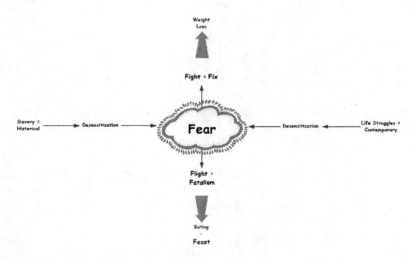

Figure 13.1 Fear—The Catalyst.

88   Emerging Theory

degree, had similar responses when overwhelmed with problems. Livia stated, for example, "but because I'm bone to bone with my knee, and everybody said, well you should exercise, but when you're hurting every day, that's really not an option. So, I know I need to; I probably should force myself." Livia states that she does not exercise because of her debilitating knee problems. However, she also admitted that she could do more. Ultimately, Livia, like Arianna, focused on the more pressing issue, her knees, and to a lesser degree on her T2DM.

Regardless of the reason for the desensitization, it took the perception of frightening news to move the participants from lethargy to a decision concerning T2DM. Thus, as a catalyst, fear evoked one of the two actions taken by the COGIC members with T2DM, and each of them depended on perceptions. As previously noted, only the announcement of T2DM struck the fear necessary for Carlos to change, which he did by dieting and exercising. On the other hand, Nick had all the classic symptoms of T2DM due to uncontrolled diabetes. However, he did not reach the status of fear until his doctor said he was a candidate for a heart attack or a stroke.

In both cases, when the fight or flight processes arose from enough fear, both chose to fight by fixing the problem. The participants gave other examples of those in the COGIC with T2DM that chose the flight option of fatalism by continuing to eat foods detrimental to their health. The best example comes from Livia's dad. About him, she said, "My dad got out of the hospital; he said God had gave him all the years that he promised. He was going to eat what he wanted, and he did just that." Nick had a similar experience with his dad. He said, "Yeah, he'd get out of the hospital, continuing to eat like he was, he'd revert back to what he was doing, he's back on insulin, back on pills and ultimately it took him out."

Fear as Factors

The participants mentioned or had experience with factors that evoked fear enough to make final decisions concerning their status that resulted in the catalytic reaction of fixes or fatalism (see Figure 13.2). Carlos said, "You can lose your limbs, lose your eyesight and kidney damage." Concerning a T2DM medication, Nick said it "could cause weight gain." Similarly, Glenn said:

> I've heard that medicine would mess you up if you be on it long, so that's why I want to get off of it if you can, you know, but I could do what I want to do what I can to get off of it.

In each case, the impending threat produced sufficient fear in the participants to attempt to fix the problem. However, fear did not always translate into solving the problem, as seen in the next section.

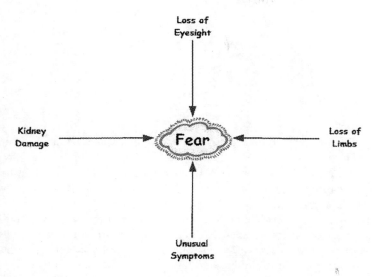

Figure 13.2 Fear Factors.

Fear as Affectivity

Although the fear factors previously mentioned had a predictable reaction of solving or fixing the problem, certain factors had the opposite effect, as seen in Figure 13.3. Once understood, these impacts also have some level of predictability. An essential ingredient was whether the participant felt like their object of the fear provided a reason to hope for improvement. The occasions mentioned in the previous "Factors" section came with avenues to escape the dreaded conditions. In other words, the causation of fear came with hope, despite the shock, and the participant would attempt to fix the problem. However, when overwhelmed, a fatalistic sense of hopelessness developed. For example, Carlos gave a scenario containing COGIC African-Americans' perception of hopelessness when he said:

> You know, we burying them too early, so this is one of the ways we do it here at this church is periodically like my wife happened to be over what we call…and she's had hospice directors that have came in and talked 'cause it's taboo in the Black community, hospice is death and not realizing that these people can help you.

The obvious conclusion is that COGIC African-Americans with T2DM think that visits from hospice are a sign that death is soon to follow. This demarcation is a signal to prepare mentally for the inevitable death. This indicator would likely explain the thoughts of the researcher's

90 *Emerging Theory*

Figure 13.3 FEAR Affectivity.

mother-in-law, who died within a year after hospice visitations began. This mental preparation was the idea of Livia concerning her dad saying, "God had gave him all the years that he promised. He was going to eat what he wanted, and he did just that." Her dad, a COGIC member with T2DM, took a fatalistic view because of his age.

This case gives another factor, age that caused these with T2DM to take a fatalistic course concerning health care. For example, when Livia talked of her dad's decision, she spoke in a tone of voice that suggested an admiration for some noble act. The fact is, this sense of nobility in choosing an avenue of defiance or escape increased as the participants aged. Livia discloses her feeling that many diseases experienced in her church in the elderly population, including diabetes, extends from exaggerated claims from the medical profession. She stated:

> And it's just to me, just from growing up in this church, I seen more—and this is back when my mom was probably my age, I seen more diabetes now than I've ever seen in my life. I didn't see this when I was a little girl running around in the church, and my mom was my age. You didn't see; I see more sickness now than I've ever seen in my life. And if it ain't diabetes, it's still all connected with— it really comes together, the hypertension, the diabetes, the sleep apnea and you have a stroke, heart disease, it's just all in there.

Livia followed this statement and stated, "They keep lowering the blood sugar levels. So, if they keep lowering the blood sugar levels, everybody in this world going to be a diabetic." Therefore, her defiance is an act of faith or belief that T2DM and other diseases are the results of the medical community having ulterior motives for declaring that older adults have these diseases. In other words, even though Livia is part of the medical community, she does not trust everything the medical community has to say, especially to the elderly.

Another ingredient that results in fatalism is simply an urge to continue eating familiar foods they enjoyed when the symptoms of T2DM are not approaching death. Livia's husband is a typical example; she said, "trying to be the perfect wife or whatever and you can see the disgust on his face, no fried chicken, do you know what I mean?" As stated earlier,

Fear and Ancestral Mentors 91

Nick also exhibited this type of defiance up to the point of his doctor, declaring he was a candidate for a heart attack or stroke. In Nick's case, youth and a sense of invincibility led to fatalism. In summary, fear factors resulted in, fixes, but the feeling of hopelessness, advanced age, distrust, and a desire for comfort foods led to fatalistic views.

Social Constructs and Knowledge

Mentors

Mentors played a vital role in the decision-making processes of managing T2DM within the COGIC members' community. Those decisions resulted in three categories: fix, faith, or fatalism. As seen in Figure 13.4, participants chose to listen to those within their social constructs who shared in their experience or who had encounters with T2DM. They used them as models or as an assist in living with the condition. The first persons given the social status of respect based on their knowledge or experience with T2DM were the ancestors of the participants.

Ancestors as Mentors

In Glenn's case, his experience with T2DM began as a child as he stated, "Grandmother gets shot, shooting herself in the thigh, and I didn't know what it was all about, you know what I'm saying?" Carlos presented several models of ancestral learning here as examples:

> He was probably old enough to be her daddy, but she died in her early 60s because she was overweight and so to me, that could have been prevented. My dad was active. I had an uncle; he died in his early 60s, overweight. Him and my dad had similar jobs. They both came, from…to…as migrant workers. My dad was older than he was, but then they got a job at the…and they started out as janitors, both of them, both of them being janitors. My dad became a diesel

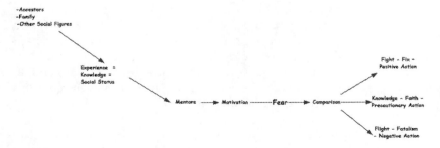

Figure 13.4 Afro-Theistic Change Agents.

mechanic, and then I think he became an electrician. And so, they went from working hard, to hardly working at all, but when my dad comes home, always in the garden. After I get home from school, I hurry up and get out of the house, before he got home, or I'm going to be working. But then when my uncle come home, get on the TV or get on the couch watching TV, "man ain't doing nothing." *I got real life examples here.* [Emphasis added] My dad kept active, and he died when he was 85. Couch potato, he dies when he is 63.

Even as the researcher reflected upon his mother's encounter with T2DM, so did all but one of the responders refer or make comparisons to their parents. Glenn stated, "I seen it with my grandmother and some others and stuff, they're talking about oh if you get your foot cut, don't get your foot cut if you have diabetes." Livia said, "It makes me wonder 'cause like my dad was diagnosed at 70-something years old as a diabetic." Carlos, "My dad's aunt...she was a diabetic, and she was overweight, and my dad, on the other hand, he always stayed busy." Finally, Nick stated, "I saw my dad die from complications of diabetes." As a reminder, this connection to the past relates to Chapter 4's discussion of the COGIC beginning and the postreconstruction establishment of African-American subcultures.

Family as Mentors

Closely related to the ancestors were family members with T2DM that influence the decisions of the participants. These family members consisted of their spouse and siblings. Although most of these have T2DM, all of them served as mentors in the participants' decisions concerning the disease.

SPOUSE AS A MENTOR

Already mentioned are Livia's concerns, frustration, and admiration of her husband, who also suffers from T2DM. She also revealed her husband's dependence upon her for his meals. This kind of dependency was a common theme among men with T2DM. Somehow the expression of love and respect for one another came through the meals prepared by the wife and enjoyed by the husband. Livia stated of her dad, "he said God had gave him all the years that he promised. He was going to eat what he wanted, and he did just that." Carlos dependent upon his nondiabetic wife's empathy in managing T2DM and specified:

> I'm not turning it down, so she was part of the problem, so now I've got to change her. My thing was again; I wasn't going to the dietitian or anything like that.

I just said, well what I want to do is, during the week, I just want to eat vegetables and then I eat meat or what have you, and I said on the weekend, I eat my starches, and that's how I did it.

Although Carlos realized his wife's meals were detrimental to his health, he continued to eat them. He displayed his dependence upon her to help manage his T2DM by altering the preparation of their meals. Livia expresses this recognition of her husband's reliance upon her by asserting, "And my sweet stuff...I don't make a habit of doing that because of my husband, more so than me. I worry more so about him." Livia specifically identifies the hindrance to change as the foods they ate. She recalled:

I know after Tuesday night, we had the thing on diabetes and then, so I went back and told my husband how good the—I call it the little seminar, was. And I really wish he had been here, and I said, okay, I made up my mind, you will not get bacon or sausage or grits or eggs this morning.

The meals eaten together by husband and wife are clear expressions of love for one another and relates changes to dislike for one another. However, Livia's attendance at a T2DM support group session expressed the need for both spouses in the COGIC community to attend and the motivation it gives to make changes without threatening that relationship.

SIBLINGS AS MENTORS

Nick mentioned several family members that he used as examples in his decision-making processes concerning T2DM.

I've seen it in my family; I've seen it with me, and I've seen where if you get control of it, you can turn some things around. If you're way too late, I'm not sure you can turn it around. If you look at my brother and his condition...I went to see him a couple weeks ago and literally his feet; they look like a football.

Livia reflects:

I just felt like, my two brothers, they was diagnosed first, and then my sister was diagnosed, and I would get on her and get on her, and I'm like, because I was fine, just like sleep apnea, I was diagnosed with sleep apnea, and I'm like, I don't have it. It's not going to happen to me, but next thing you know, they say I have sleep apnea, and I have diabetes and—but, you know, even with that, like I said,

> I never had a low reaction. I know what a low reaction is 'cause my husband is a diabetic, one of the worst kind and so they put me on Metformin. They said 1,000 milligrams and I told them at that time; I said I'm not taking that, not taking 1,000. I said I'll take 500, so that's pretty much what I've been taking.

Carlos recalled, "I knew my two brothers had it, but I got a sister, and she's real secretive, she don't tell her business, but she want to know all your business and come to find out, she had it." These individuals use their siblings as an example to motivate each other, as seen in the next example. Over multiple paragraphs, Nick stated, "And the whole while my dad would say you're digging your grave one fork at a time. He would say that about himself. And that's what he did. I shared that with my brother and sister now."

Other Social Figures as Mentors

Responders also used athletes, pastors, doctors, and church members in the decision-making process concerning diabetes management. For example, Carlos developed a dietary plan that worked for him based on an athlete he heard on television and used him as a mentor. Carlos elaborates:

> I cut that out, and I start drinking a lot of water...I got this from just watching TV when Shaquille O'Neal lost all that weight...He had said, when they ask him how he lost the weight, he say he started eating more, so that got my attention...I want that, this will work for me, and what he was saying, your body is like a car, and you got to keep gas in the car and what we do and this is what I was guilty of. Okay, I might eat breakfast, and I can eat nothing till lunch, so I'm getting hungry, so at lunch, you eat more than you should and then when you eat lunch, by the time you get home, dinner you have ate nothing between lunch and dinner. You get home and again, you pig out some more, and that end up hurting you and what you're supposed to do, eat some snacks in between and so you never get hungry. So, what I start doing there, I would take some fruit or whatever, I eat my breakfast before I leave. Maybe 2 or 3 hours later, I get me some fruit and lunchtime come, in between lunch and dinner, get me some more—you know, something, nothing with sugar, nothing like that, something just to keep me from being hungry and then at night, same thing, fruit or something and I did that.

The participants also listen and trust their pastor to a degree in matters concerning their health. Glenn stated, "I listen to the church and listen to the pastor and stuff." Arianna said, "But like, when the Pastor asked us to fast not long ago, I didn't fast the full length of time he said, but I did fast some." Carlos observed, "So our pastor has allowed since we have healthcare professionals here in the church and as a matter of fact, his daughter is one, and so he's allowed different ones to come in and kind of educate the people...."

Finally, the participants listen to their doctors and other Christians who stressed the need to make changes. For example, in continuation of Nick's statement in the last section, he detailed, "I heard Dr. Peter saying that diabetic medication when you start taking it; it starts affecting your organs, your body, your lungs, brain, heart, kidneys... when I go back, [I want] for him to tell me get off it." Concerning Christians, Carlos concluded that all should model healthy living. Saying:

> We as Christians ~ we need to be an example ~ we need to do the best ~ we need to be the best we can be ~ and so we don't make the name of Christ ~ where they say well those Christians. You know ~ I don't want to be like that, I won't, you know go in those workplaces or a place, be the best I can be.

14 Emergent Categories
Fix, Fatalism, Faith, Frustration, and Authoritarian Mentors

This chapter continues the unfolding of the categories as they were revealed during the analysis. The participants used ancestors, family members, and others from their social constructs to make decisions concerning type 2 diabetes mellitus (T2DM). These individuals provided an experience that produced knowledge and gave them social status deemed worthy of the participants' attention. Therefore, they served as mentors and motivated the participants to make a decision. This motivation resulted from fear, as discussed in the previous chapter. However, the result of the decisions was not unilateral or ubiquitous because the participants use mentors to make comparisons before selecting a course of action. In other words, the participants sometimes changed categories based on additional comparison and fears exhibited in the previous chapter.

Category 2: Fix

Through "comparative" measures, the participants made one of the three decisions concerning their T2DM. Although the fear of catastrophe was the primary reason COGIC members with T2DM chose the positive action of fixing the problem, their health was not always the main concern. For example, Nick quantified, "It made me change my life and my family, my son's, my wife, my granddaughter, hope that she doesn't. There's generations that are diabetic in my family." In other words, his motivation was reversing the effects and trends exhibited in his family now and in the future. Howbeit, most feared the ravaging effects of T2DM on their bodies, as seen in previous examples. Presented earlier were cases where Carlos feared the adverse impact of diabetes on his body and even death that motivated him to diet and exercise to fix his problems with T2DM.

Category 3: Fatalism

In opposition to positive action, negative action or fatalism resulted from comparisons and a conclusion that the evidence refuted the notion of T2DM. The participants are not living in denial; rather, they conduct an independent study and compare the results with their knowledge of T2DM. When the evidence did not match their concept of T2DM, the participants decided to dismiss the doctors' claim, and that decision became absolute. Seemingly, in defiance, they continued their usual dietary and exercise routine.

In Arianna's case, she seldom monitored her glucose, took the recommended medication dosages, or read information about diabetes, because she did not believe she had diabetes. She replied, "Well, when I was checking it, the numbers always looking pretty good to me, so...I just stopped." Daily monitoring of blood glucose levels is the only certain way of knowing when diabetes is not under control, which leads to severe complications of diabetes.

She goes on to say, "Some people, I guess maybe it depends on whatever. I've never had symptoms that I know of, you know or anything." Here, Arianna admits that she made her decisions based on her knowledge of symptoms exhibited by people living with diabetes. Likewise, Nick drew a similar conclusion. He said, "And I remember [dad] used to say he smelled fruit and I had never [Nick demonstrates the action of sniffing that he did when he was peeing, and then said] I don't smell that." As a result, and like other incidences of fatalism exhibited by the participants, Nick dismissed the warning signs and continued without altering his diet and exercise routine.

Category 4: Faith

The final response to comparisons made with mentors was faith-based interpretation by participants who surmised that their health was equivalent to other individuals. As a result, and unlike the fatalistic approach, they proceeded with caution and remained alert for more information or knowledge to adjust. Beliefs concerning the participants' status with T2DM was a factor for fix and fatalism. However, beliefs based on the participants' knowledge of healthy individuals, and remaining alerted to ideas, produced a different category, called faith that resulted in precautionary action. The participants were not in denial, and in fact, they were willing to concede to having diabetes.

The problem was that the doctors' diagnosis did not match their perception of T2DM, based on their current knowledge of the disease and with comparisons made with their mentors. Later, Livia stated, "I have a friend...she's not big at all...everybody can't be a diabetic...I just don't believe that." Livia's reasoned that should doctors' conclusion that her weight was the deciding factor, then why does her African-American friend have the same diagnosis. In other words, the doctor apparently left out some information vital to her understanding of T2DM. Furthermore, based on her knowledge of diabetes from a nursing background, the indicative numbers for diabetes are lower than in the past.

98   Emerging Theory

As a result, Livia exhibited disbelief and frustration with her diagnosis and did not take the recommended dosage of medication, based on her knowledge of its adverse effects. Livia continued to learn to make the best decisions on how to proceed in managing her glucose readings. However, Livia had a limitation to her inactivity based upon her fear of the worst-case scenario. She believed things could progress to the point of no return, which is code for imminent death. She declared,

> Don't feel an effect, you know, we're not using losing eyesight, we still can see, we still got our legs, so we feel like whatever. But then, when that sucker-punch hit us, then we may have a massive stroke that can't be reversed.

Consequently, Livia admitted that regardless of her view of having T2DM, she acted to prevent the onset of a "sucker punch" that she believed led to death.

Therefore, the participants' belief about their T2DM status based on a comparison to mentors resulted in positive action, negative action, or precautionary action. In each case, fear and knowledge were deciding factors in response to the diagnosis of diabetes. In summary, fear and disbelief concerning the participants' status with T2DM emerged as factors that produced the fix and fatalism categories, whereas faith based on knowledge of healthy individuals resulted in precautionary action by making comparisons to mentors.

Dualism: Doctors or Pastors as Mentors

Doctors and pastors, as mentors in the social interactions of the participants, emerged as having significant roles that helped or hindered the participant decisions concerning diabetes management. Each contributed in differing ways of fixing or taking fatalistic approaches to the management of his or her T2DM. Howbeit, the doctors' interactions with the participants had the most direct impact on the decisions made toward diabetes management, while pastors had the most indirect effect.

The most desperate responses were polarized in the action of fixing the problem or for various reasons, taking a fatalistic approach that results in negative or no action toward reducing the effects of T2DM. Along the way, fear, faith, and frustration were also solidified as categories while surrendering, and solutions emerged as processes. Although Figure 13.4 depicts linear progression, in reality, they were more complicated and only completely revealed when considering the entire social constructs of the participants concerning T2DM, as seen in Part 6. Also, the participants' knowledge of T2DM did not emerge as a category, but as an intricate part of their social constructs and interactions. Figure 14.1 depicts doctors and pastors' interactions with the participants that produce

Emergent Categories 99

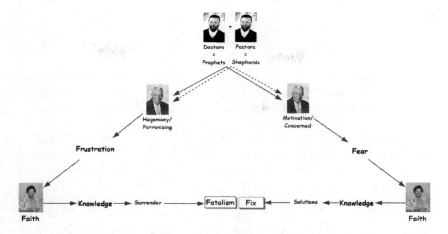

Figure 14.1 Dualistic Afro-Theistic Faith, Knowledge, and Social Constructs.

one of the two results. Howbeit, the means of getting to each are fragile, complex, and sometimes involved the same individual.

Doctors as Mentors

Two clear examples, as mentioned in Chapter 11 (see Figure 11.1), under symbolic interactionism, are the medical and church ministers, or doctors and pastors. Depending on the perception of the participants, either could cause a participant to fix or neglect their problems with T2DM. The participants similarly viewed the doctor's role as their pastor, as one sent from God. For example, Carlos declared:

> We're made in the image of God. God is creative and so; a part of God is in us and so, I mean, look at man. Look at all the great things man has done. He's put these people [doctors] here for a reason, and so, faith is one thing but man, don't be stupid. You know what I'm saying? Go see the doctor.

Carlos argues that COGIC individuals with diabetes should overcome their fear of the news from doctors and let them use their gifts of healing in managing T2DM. Thus, Carlos revealed his and COGIC members' perception of the dual role of physicians. On the one hand, they feared the hegemonic announcement of doom. More accurately, participants viewed doctors' specific role as one holding a ministerial office like that of a prophet. COGIC members understand prophets in the Bible as those able to predict the future and give advice on avoiding pending doom. On the other hand, participants welcomed doctors in mentoring and a caring role of healing.

Obviously, Carlos felt hegemony and the callous prophecy of the doctors, lamenting:

> My primary care physician, he wasn't too—what's the word I'm looking for?
> He really wasn't a good cheerleader because all the time he was telling me well, you going to get it…So he wasn't a cheerleader, pretty much prophesied that one day, of course, he was right.

Nick revealed the patronizing tone of his doctor, stating, "He'd be like well your blood sugar went up a little bit, but I'm sure you'll bring it down. I was good with it." In both cases, the doctor minimized Carlos and Nick's concerns for their condition. The doctor lessened the participants' belief about the seriousness of their diabetes and served to frustrate their efforts against T2DM. This minimizing created a domino effect that included surrendering to conditions as seen in their fatalistic lapse in dietary and exercise discipline. As expected, their diabetes worsened.

Conversely, the participants perceived doctors as mentors when they show them respect. Glenn expressed this felt respect to his new doctor when he stated:

> But the doctor that I have now…he do set down and talk to me like you talking to me and had to tell him, man, I sure appreciate you telling me that, but you know, the doctor that I had years before that, you know that doctor…I tell you what the doctor I got now stayed in that room with me longer the first time, longer than my other doctor did, three to four years.

Carlos perceived his doctor's respect when he was forthright with "fear factors." He stated:

> And again, especially with people who have grown up in Church of God and Christ, Holiness churches, a lot of times to me, probably the better motivation tactic is the fear factor. So, maybe they start showing people look, this is what can happen to you. You can lose your limbs, lose your eyesight and kidney damage 'cause I know when I was a kid, as a matter of fact, diabetes, that was a term that came later. In fact, when I was a kid, it was sugar. I'm like, that didn't sound too bad to me, sounds pretty sweet, you know what I'm saying? So it's no fear. Our culture, you know, I mean back then they preached fire and brimstone, it's fear factor.

In Nick's case, the fear factor came when his doctor said, "Oh my god! She said you're a candidate for a heart attack or stroke." Ironically, the fear factors are also prophetic, but the perception of the blunt messages was one of respect for a mentor or someone concerned about the participants' health. In a cascade, fear alerted the participants to the imminent danger from T2DM, and with this understanding, the participants worked on solutions to fix their problems.

Moreover, the participants were sensitive to hegemonic incidences that resembled prejudice. Glenn mentioned his perception of his first doctor:

> He wasn't only doing me like that, and I don't know whether a lot of Blacks I talked to he was turning them around real quick. My uncle was going to him, going to him regular, come to find out my uncle had emphysema…[his] Sister…had told him…you need to change your doctor because that doctor ain't listening. Come to find out, my uncle had all kinds of diseases and stuff and died.

The disrespect Glenn felt from his doctor hindered his ability to manage his diabetes, not because he did not trust his doctor, and he did not, but because his doctor withheld vital information. Glenn continually asked questions during the interview to fill in missing knowledge. Therefore, Glenn could not avoid fatalism with his first doctor because the physician withheld knowledge. As seen when Glenn said, "One time, they [doctors] did have me thinking just White people couldn't get it, diseases like diabetes and high blood pressure." Glenn did not have a problem with White doctors as seen above; the problem was his observation of the physician's attitude toward him. Nick appreciated having an African-American physician, but ultimately, the perception of the participants toward their doctors made the difference in managing T2DM. Nick demonstrated the importance of message delivery over the race of the physician by connecting two lines of transcriptions:

> I just always knew it [exercise]was good for you, and she had told me, the doctor, she was an African doctor, and she told me exercise would help lower it [blood glucose]…She tried to teach me, but you know being young like I was, it was really going in one ear, out the other.

Notice, Nick respected the doctor but ultimately ignored her instructions. On the other hand, the White female doctor in the above paragraph entirely commanded his attention with her shocking announcement of imminent danger. Finally, the respect and forthrightness from doctors that the participants expect from messages in their African-American COGIC churches make their belief about T2DM an Afro-Theistic belief or faith.

Pastors as Mentors

Pastors' dual roles were less apparent because concern and mentoring dominated their position, but the participants revealed the existence of hegemony. As Sheppard's lead, their flocks of sheep, the title of pastor assumes role modeling and special care for the members of their congregation. Unexpectedly, the participants identified a hegemonic side to this leadership that leads their flock to a fatalistic approach to managing T2DM.

Glenn hinted at this hegemony when he said, "You know what I'm saying? I give them [pastors] respect and stuff, you understand what I'm saying, but I know they can tell me to have faith in this and that, but they've got to have it too." Glenn, a new member of the COGIC church, had not learned the aforementioned "code," "Touch not my anointed and do not my prophet in a harm" when he pointed out the obvious.

Perhaps his newness as a member of the COGIC church also explains his uninhibited view of doctors' failures. The fact is only one other participant dared, though reverently, to point out the hegemonic side of the COGIC ministry, and that was another minister. Carlos stated:

> I think a lot of church, where ministers go, they won't touch their stuff because you noticed in our church, the preachers are the biggest, they're some of the biggest...obese people in the church. Most people don't preach on their self. You know, it's not necessarily right. You stay away from subjects like that; it's going to make you look bad...and so how do I preach on temperance when I'm on the pulpit weighing 269 pounds? I'm not messing with that subject.

Therefore, this hegemonic process is by way of omission. As a result, COGIC members are not receiving the customary "fire and brimstone" messages when it comes to ones against diabetes. This omission results in fatalism for members with T2DM for the same reasons Glenn in the previous section experienced it from his doctor who withheld vital information. This indirect impact may be worse than the direct effects of physicians because of the multiple weekly interactions with participants with T2DM with their pastors. By implication, pastors, especially those obese who through omission of messages on the contribution of obesity to T2DM, will lead members into the same fatalistic condition.

Concerning Frustration

This chapter and the previous one treated the categories and stakeholders in the natural way they emerged. In other words, the hearing of how the participants related to T2DM took precedence over the extraction of the categories from their dialogue. For example, frustration is not treated as a separate category in this chapter, as was fear, in the previous chapter, and faith, fix, and fatalism, in this chapter, but mentioned throughout in context and emerges naturally from the central category of substantive living, in the next chapter (Chapter 15). Likewise, although the enlightening and needed theory that began to emerge in the next chapter will ultimately achieve the goal of the study, it does so methodically. That is, it follows the same order and natural progression where the participants inform the researcher of the theory to develop as it connects previous findings with new understanding and moves the study closer to the sought-after grounded theory.

15 Anatomy of Substantive Living

Five categories emerged in capturing the actions, interactions, and emotions that resulted from the social constructs of the African-American Church of God in Christ (COGIC) members with type 2 diabetes mellitus (T2DM). Integrated into this chapter are these five categories, previously mentioned, where all but one had an expanded introduction. However, now, they are fully developed into a theoretical explanation grounded in the data from the participants' processes of actions, interactions, and emotions that extend from one core theme of Afro-Theism. This fundamental idea necessarily connects to each concept and explains the knowledge-based decisions made concerning living and dying with T2DM that emerged from the hypothesis made through inductive reasoning. The evaluation of data, especially the knowledge-based decision-making incidences, revealed a desire for the participants to have a fulfilling life, whether it meant a shorter life or longer one became secondary. Following is the process of the anatomy of discovering the "permeated learning" theory from "substantive living," the core category and illustrating the desire of having and doing what these participants had enjoyed after years of cultivating those behaviors. Shown below is how faith, knowledge, and social constructs concerning T2DM produced the actions, interactions, and emotions. Throughout the process (taking years), the participants defined or redefined their meaning of substantive living based on what they had learned, as manifested in adjustments within what they now believed, or their "faith."

Figure 15.1 is a composite matrix that unveils the coveted processes or actions, interactions, and the emotions of the participants. The diagrams merit attention to details, such as the direction and thickness of arrows, since they capture the essence of the discussion and are critical intimate parts of the theory developed. Interestingly, the actions and emotions evolved into five categories, while an interaction fittingly made a connection to each. Faith, fear, fix, frustration, and fatalism emerged from the participants' data as fluctuating categories of actions and interactions, illustrated in the diagram, each with a stimulus of interaction and the consequence of moving to a different category. Fortuitously, but fittingly forming the shape of a cross is the axis of actions and emotions

Anatomy of Substantive Living 105

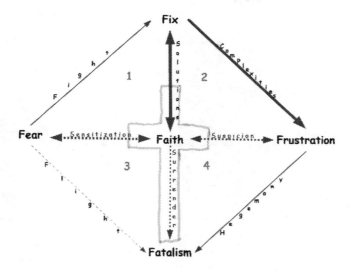

Figure 15.1 Afro-Theistic Substantive Living.

with faith serving as a hub. Fear and frustration identify the emotions, left-to-right; while fix and fatalism are the actions, in a top-to-bottom symmetry, and faith being the heart of what the participants believe about T2DM causing one of four directional moves. Furthermore, like the symbolic interactionism of Figure 11.1, there also exist left-to-right and top-to-bottom symmetry in Figure 15.1.

Congruent to symbolic interactionism in Chapter 11 (see Figure 11.1), the top half contains the more positive, and the bottom half is the more negative categories of the processes in the illustration. Ultimately, the top reveals processes of solutions and complexities to living, and the bottom is that of the participants surrendering to death. Also, like symbolic interactionism, the top half represents positive actions, and the bottom half are the negative ones. The left half expresses the emotion of fear, and the right hand represents the emotion of frustration.

Moreover, there are four quadrants (see Figure 15.1 and Table 15.1); the first (1) quadrant is a triangle that has the best outcomes in managing diabetes and the best chance to experience self-efficacy. Although the second (2) quadrant equates to diabetes management, the participants are disgruntled and less determined to continue their regiments. Participants or the examples they use that had diabetes are in the third (3) quadrant, "gave in" to harmful habits through self-will. On the other hand, those in the fourth (4) quadrant, discouraged by hegemonic overtones, "gave up" and stopped trying to manage their diabetes. The number referenced (1–4) representing each quadrant for each category (Figure 15.1) has connecting processes that vary in significance regarding quantity or the

106 Emerging Theory

Table 15.1 Code Triangulated Significance

Categorical Strength			Total	
Quadrant 1	Most Positive	1212	4088	
Quadrant 2	Less Positive	1206		
Quadrant 3	Less Negative	838		
Quadrant 4	Most Negative	832		
Interactive Strength			Total	Percentage (%)
Quadrant 2	Less Positive	275	689	17
Quadrant 1	Most Positive	241		
Quadrant 4	Most Negative	92		
Quadrant 3	Less Negative	81		

degree, and the direction of influence, as noted by the type and shading of lines and arrows.

Fascinatingly, the number of codes, as seen in Table 15.1, revealed quadrants that counterbalanced the participants' actions, interactions, and emotions within and across strengths. For example, within, Quadrant 1 opposes Quadrant 2, and Quadrant 3 opposes Quadrant 4, whether categorical (actions, emotions) or interactions. Across the strengths (categorical and interactive), the most positive actions and emotions of Quadrant 1 are countered by the less positive interactions of Quadrant 2, and this pattern continues for the remaining quadrants. There is a notable difference of 83% of the codes belonging to the categorical strengths as opposed to the much lower 17% of the interactive strengths.

Remarkably, the total number of better outcomes (2,372) is less than the less desired outcome (2,405) by 33 codes. Note, the number of codes overlap at the "cross" for the quadrants (Figure 15.1). Therefore, based on these simple mathematical calculations, the participants' categorical strengths (actions and emotions) in Table 15.1 are seen by far more often than their interactivity strengths. Practically speaking, this balance means that the best scenario for those living with diabetes, Quadrant 1, actions, and emotions, has a counterbalance with a worse action, Quadrant 2, interaction, poised to oppose it. Moreover, the balance slightly favors actions and emotions that are more damaging (less positive), which works against optimism, possibly hinting at the reason for poor management of diabetes of the one in three African-Americans.

Nevertheless, the interactions (interactive strengths) of Table 15.1, which indicates change, occurs much less frequently and therefore lessens the likelihood or frequency of changes toward the overall "negative" Quadrants 3 and 4 (Figure 15.1), both running the risk of "fatalism," as the course of action. In other words, whatever the action or emotion, overall the good (Quadrants 1 and 2) outweighs the bad (Quadrants 3 and 4) and change from that status is slow. So, based on the number of codes (Table 15.1), people with diabetes will linger in or maintain a more positive or less positive status most of the time (Figure 15.1). That is, whether "more" or "less," the positive interactions (Quadrants 1 and 2) more than double the negative ones (Quadrants 3 and 4) in Table 15.1.

The triangulated (multiplicity of sources) significance of the codes reveals a certain balance that helps explain the complexities in understanding how African-Americans in the COGIC church manage their diabetes. In the following sections through the identity of 1,423 of the 1,571 codes, and elucidated through memos and the presented diagrams, five categories, and other processes emerged from the participants' data. The additional 143 remains unspecified since they added no new information, to prevent unnecessarily forcing data into compartments. The order of presentation begins with the dominant concept, faith, and culminates with the overarching "substantive living" that connects to all categories.

Faith

Faith, located in the center of the theoretical model (Figure 15.1), stands for the symbolic interactionism or the perception of the participants concerning T2DM. This symbolic interaction expands on the perceptions leading to promotion and distractions of health in Figure 11.1, now identifiable as faith (belief) about diabetes. The codes connecting faith to T2DM is an extraction from data relating to the participants' beliefs about diabetes, actions, interactions, and emotions concerning the disease. Nonetheless, faith is the most prominent and complex category of the five. Mysteriously, the number of codes that identify each of the five categories (Table 15.2) far exceeds the number of codes that connects one category to another, identified as one category "to" another category. However, the sheer number of nonconnecting codes easily reduced to five groups of related codes unequivocally identified these five groups as categories.

Nevertheless, the identification of "faith," which the literature review suggested would be part of the African-American culture, was not straightforward and put the entire research in jeopardy. So much so that the researcher became extremely lightheaded when the following took place in the very first interview. Surprised with push back when the researcher attempted to imposed a combined researched and self-defined understanding of faith, the participants countered with vehement expressions indicating that faith and diabetes did not have any relationship. The suggestion seemed repugnant and astonishing to them. This embarrassment resulted in having the participants both define faith and inform the researcher of the ways it may apply. As a result, even asking

108 *Emerging Theory*

the participants for a definition and application surprised all except Arianna, who denied having diabetes based on her understanding, in the first place. She volunteered for this study based on her doctor's estimate, the one who stated that she had diabetes. Therefore, her definition of faith related to T2DM distilled into a matter of believing or not

Table 15.2 Afro-Theistic Processes: Code Statistics

Category	Faith	Fix	Fear	Frustration	Fatalism	Total
Nick	83	191	86	14	13	387
Carlos	78	115	27	22	14	256
Livia	84	61	27	62	14	248
Glenn	86	56	22	52	8	224
Arianna	15	2	2	8	0	27
Subtotal—categorical codes	346	425	164	158	49	1,142
Substantive living relationships	275	1	1	1	3	281
Totals	621	426	165	159	52	**1,423**
Category Percentages (%)	44	30	12	11	4	

Actions, Interactions, Emotions	Total	Percentage (%)
Faith	621	
Faith to Fix	65	10
Faith to Fear	38	6
Faith to Fatalism	32	5
Faith to Frustration	31	5
Fix	426	
Fix to Faith	111	26
Fix to Frustration	63	15
Fear	165	
Fear to Fix	24	15
Fear to Fatalism	8	5
Fear to Faith	3	2
Frustration	159	
Frustration to Fatalism	24	15
Frustration to Faith	5	3
Fatalism	52	

Anatomy of Substantive Living

404 Interactions Total	
Total	Percent (%)
Faith and Fix	
176	44
Fix and Frustration	
63	16
Faith and Fear	
41	10
Faith and Frustration	
36	9
Faith and Fatalism	
32	8
Fear and Fix	
24	6
Frustration and Fatalism	
24	6
Fear and Fatalism	
8	5

believing she had the disease. Importantly, all the participants, except Carlos, expressed doubt about having diabetes at some point. Strikingly, T2DM seemed so private that thoughts of their spiritual life and physical status having a connection never occurred. If that was true, then the research was over or must change completely, since the referenced literature in this study connected faith and diabetes, at least nominally, with African-Americans. Therefore, the quest became the discovery of this connection and the reason for such a thorough investigation and prominent part of this study, as the following reveals.

Again, most sobering was the irritation with the request to define faith concerning diabetes, which required careful analysis of the data to uncover the definition. For example, Carlos said, "Faith is one thing but man, don't be stupid." Here, Carlos views faith in one biblical sense of expecting God to bring about the desired results miraculously. When he said, "don't be stupid," he meant God had given those with diabetes the ability to take action. Therefore, claiming to be waiting for Him to do it based on having faith is stupid. Notwithstanding, he did not claim faith and diabetes were mutually exclusive; rather, faith must not exclude the participant's ability to act. Nick had a similar reaction but clarified the type of faith suitable for COGIC members with T2DM. He specified:

> God put some responsibility on us. Just because we have faith doesn't say I still can eat a quart or pint of ice cream...Sometimes I think

we're ignorant and in denial that I can beat this on faith when God is daily giving you an understanding, this isn't good for you; don't eat it.

Nick equates faith and diabetes with absurdity when expecting God to take care of the diabetes sufferer's responsibilities. However, he stated that the type of faith COGIC members with diabetes needed is one that combines it with restraint, responsibility, and intelligence.

Livia also shows her strong objection to the notion of an association between faith and diabetes. However, she left reason to believe her objection resulted from the novelty of the idea. She detailed, "I guess I haven't. I don't really—I don't think I have because like I say, I just really feel like this wouldn't happen to me, and I don't think I associate the two together." She concluded that since she did not believe she had diabetes, there was no reason to consider her faith. Howbeit, she left room for the possibility of another definition of faith when she said, "I don't think I associate the two together."

On the other hand, Glenn demonstrated his understanding of the multiple meanings of faith when he asked, "What faith you're talking about." Based on his question, he surmised that the definition of faith varied based on the context or the circumstance of application. Earlier, Glenn showed the same objections that others had when thinking of faith as placing the responsibility of managing T2DM on God. He said:

> No, but common sense tells you that you should have faith and rely on God, and you apply yourself to it, God is only going to do so much, you've got to do something too. I listen to the church and listen to the pastor and stuff, but then I got common sense for myself, you know, to understand the Bible as much as I can and try to and you know, I ask questions if I don't understand something, you know.

Glenn states that faith in the context of T2DM is a collaborative effort between God and COGIC members with diabetes. In managing diabetes, those affected by the disease can only expect God to do things beyond their capability. However, most of the responsibilities belong to the one who has diabetes, and their faith should be such that it is *active, advisable, teachable, practical,* and *searches* for answers. Glenn associated faith concerning diabetes with doing what knowledge about diabetes instructed him and the ones preaching about faith's responsibility to do likewise when he said:

> You know what I'm saying? I give them respect and stuff, you understand what I'm saying, but I know they can tell me to have faith in this and that, but they've got to have it too.

Anatomy of Substantive Living 111

Therefore, in Glenn's estimate of faith, based on his statements, it is doing what knowledge, which he called common sense, instructs one to do. Ironically, even Livia's belief about her diabetes status is part of the participants' definition of faith. Ultimately, the data revealed three components to the definition of faith about T2DM. Initially, the participants' beliefs about diabetes dominated the definition because every participant had beliefs and doubts about having diabetes. Next, each took actions or made decisions based on knowledge about T2DM. Furthermore, more than one expressed the belief that God expected them to take responsibility and manage their diabetes. Meaning, faith is the participants' beliefs about diabetes linked with their emotions, actions taken, if any, based on multiple sources of knowledge from social constructs and God's help. A more concise composite definition of *faith* from the participants is,

> COGIC members with T2DM responding with knowledge based on their beliefs about diabetes and relying on God for circumstances beyond their control.

Additionally, faith emerged as the hub that connected to all other categories in both degree and direction. Regarding quantity, 44% of the 1,423 codes (Table 15.2) for the five categories belongs to faith. Regarding direction, the next four sections speak of faith's influence on the other four categories. Although the faith of the participants influences each of the categories, the primary direction is the actions and emotions toward it.

Finally, all concepts have two components: the influence of their social constructs and changes in knowledge through reflection, which identifies the contexts and the basis of the processes or actions of those with T2DM. Statistically, nearly 75% of the overwhelming number of codes (621) relates to faith or the participants' quest to understand what a diagnosis of diabetes meant. The fundamental belief is that the cause and cure of diabetes lie in the gain and loss of weight. Typical is what Carlos remarks when he states:

> And I look at my brothers, they all overweight. You know, some of my family has it, but it may be genetics or what have you, but to me. I mean he was—now I'm bigger than I should be, but I'm moving, and I don't think it's a coincidence that the exercise and the loss of the weight, that now I don't have it.

Carlos denotes the reliance on his family's history for making comparisons for understanding his condition. As discussed earlier, ancestors is another facet and the primary source of knowledge about diabetes that influences the participants' belief or faith concerning their T2DM status.

112   *Emerging Theory*

The next source of this knowledge is their clinicians. Livia states, "Well, lose weight, lose weight, I hear that 24/7 and you know, get my eating under control." Combining these cases reflects the participants' method of understanding T2DM through the triangulation (multiplicity of sources) of data, primarily their unique circumstances, observational field notes, and repeatedly listening to their taped interviews. From these sources came convincing evidence that their major concern was their weight and its connection with diabetes.

Faith-to-Fix

The significant influence of faith (see Table 15.2) upon another category was through the process called solutions. It purposed to "fix" a problem (see Figure 15.1) experienced by those with T2DM. Coding revealed that these influences came through social constructs and the knowledge of the participants.

Social Constructs

A typical example of faith influencing a fix through social constructs is Glenn. He states:

> Like what you saying about a second opinion, that would be good too, you know, instead of just telling you, say hey—even they have classes you go to and like telling you, showing you what you should eat or whatever, you know, stuff like that too, you know.

In the cited case, Glenn acknowledges the benefit of gaining knowledge through the social construct of diabetes education classes. Notice his recent rant against hegemonic overtones and the preference of demonstration, through support groups, for example.

Knowledge

Nick was motivated to change or fix his problems with diabetes through his past and present familial knowledge. He stated:

> Certain things what changed me was thinking about my dad did insulin, my brother who will be 58 tomorrow; he's in worst shape than my father was...he got edema. Yeah, its big, he's in the hospital now going on three months. Yeah, his legs are turning dark. But, he was one who decided, ate what he wanted. I'd watch my father go in the hospital with complications of diabetes. Within a month they took him off insulin and took him off pills 'cause he was eating what they told him.

Anatomy of Substantive Living 113

Nick expressed a variety of emotions and concerns, which led him taking preventive measures. However, this action or attempt to "fix" his problem resulted from the "knowledge" he gained through his social constructs.

Faith-to-Fear

Faith's influence upon the action of fear ranks second behind that of fixing the problem (see Table 15.2) for those with T2DM through processes of sensitization. Sensitization is becoming aware through social constructs, knowledge, or experience that results in fear. The means of sensitization resulting in fear is from the knowledge that changes a belief related to T2DM and incites fear.

Social Constructs

Regarding social constructs, faith connects to fear through processes of sensitization. Being sensitized is the exposure to, in this case, causes of fear by those of the participants' social construct. Nick demonstrates how social constructs and knowledge work together. He states:

> Yeah, he told me, he said I don't want to alarm you, but I noticed that your cholesterol levels are going up. So, we'll continue to do blood work. He said I want to try to do something natural first, so he recommended red yeast rice. Red yeast rice, something natural you can take that should help you lower it. So, I started taking that, but when I walked out of his office, I was like cholesterol. I didn't know much about it but sounds like I'd been eating too much fatty foods. Yeah. So, I decided well I am gonna do something different. I'm going to cut out beef and pork and stick with chicken, fish, and turkey.

In this case, the social construct concerning T2DM is a doctor who sensitizes or made Nick aware of natural approaches to managing diabetes. However, the doctor elicited fear when he mentioned cholesterol. After reflecting on his knowledge of dietary intakes, Nick surmised that the primary sources of cholesterol were certain meats, which he decided to exclude from his diet.

Another case is when Livia states:

> My daughter say I'm a hypochondriac, which I'm not, but I know, I wake up one morning, like 146! She say, there you go, my blood sugar's up, but I want to stay like that because I want to be aware, okay, you know what you have, you know you need to leave that alone.

Livia used her social construct (family) to motivate her to stay fearful through the sensitization or daily readings of her glucose levels.

114   *Emerging Theory*

Knowledge

The case of Nick above demonstrated the interaction of social constructs with knowledge, making it difficult to separate them. Nevertheless, after the beginning, the interview with Carlos showed the faith-to-fear connection to the process of sensitization. He stated:

> As far as I know, and it has something to do with your blood. The sugar level in your blood and I do, just by seeing some of my family members who suffer with it, I know it has some adverse effects of the disease and my own self. I know that your diet, especially with type 2 diabetes, has a lot to do with it, but I don't pretend know a great deal about it, but I just know that it's something I don't want.

Although Carlos does not claim to be an expert on diabetes, he demonstrated the continual building of knowledge that keeps him sensitize enough to fear T2DM.

Faith-to-Fatalism

Another effect that faith can have is the production of fatalistic actions by those with T2DM. Completing the process came through surrendering to conditions fatalistic to those with T2DM. The process of surrendering also came through social constructs and the knowledge of those suffering from T2DM.

Social Constructs

The best illustration of a social construct resulting in fatalism through processes of surrendering came through Carlos's experiment. He stated:

> I give a workshop here every year, and so I remember doing a workshop on it and I kind of set them up a little bit, and I can't exactly remember how…one of my ways of getting people here, I always offer a free dinner. So, after the workshop, after you get the teaching, you get a free meal…And so I had already did some preliminary stuff at the beginning, and then my next line was, I had this smorgasbord place [only PowerPoint]. That's where we are on Sunday. This is what, we leave church, we done told to do this and not do that and that's where we would go, and we eat. They say all you can eat, we get our money's worth, but then we go back and preach against the cigarette smoking, the snuff and all this, but the doctor has told you not to do certain things, yet you go and do it. Now how out of control are you? So that was my opportunity to shock them because, at the time, I hadn't been through this, and that's what the Lord was

dealing me with. You can't control your flesh, see how hypocritical you're being. You know, cigarette smokers inhale, you just as bad.

Many codes came from these paragraphs, where Carlos demonstrates the necessity of shock or fear to motivate COGIC members with T2DM. Among the codes came the overwhelming temptation to surrender to the self-destructive behavior of overeating through the influences of social constructs.

Knowledge

Combining statements from a couple of paragraphs reveals Arianna's fatalistic processes of surrendering to T2DM through her knowledge. She states:

> Well, not at first, I guess because they tried, he said to watch my diet or whatever. Well, I don't know because like I say, they said I was on the borderline. So then when they got past the borderline, I guess, they put me on the Metformin…So I really never took that half in the morning, maybe a couple of times.

The paragraph above juxtapositions Arianna's disbelief that she has diabetes based on her knowledge against the clinicians' knowledge. Since she did not believe (faith) that she had diabetes, she took a fatalistic approach by modifying or completely ignoring her doctors' advice.

Faith-to-Frustration

As mentioned in the Faith-to-Fear section, another emotion experienced by those with T2DM is frustration. In this section, the route is from faith-to-frustration through the process of suspicion. The faith-to-frustration path exhibited the same two origins—social constructs and knowledge—as in previous intracategorical connections, except the process is suspicion.

Social Constructs

In several paragraphs, Livia states:

> But she said I went from 6.8 to 6.9, but still back up. Why are you fussing at me for a point? I said "ma'am, I'm a nurse. I know"…I guess she was a medical assistant.

Notice, Livia became suspicious of the claims from a medical assistant's demeaning remarks based on her knowledge of hemoglobin A_{1c} readings.

116   *Emerging Theory*

Livia perceives the condescending remarks as being hegemonic and frustrating, which led to her pushing back with her knowledge. Later comments suggest that the pushback did not extend from retaliation, but the consequences of the effects it had upon her faith or belief about her condition with which she must live.

Knowledge

Livia also gives an excellent example of faith, leading to frustration based on her understanding. She states:

> I was diagnosed, which was kind of discouraging, I was diagnosed April of last year, and that's something I said would never happen to me, and I was diagnosed. I did some routine lab work, and when it came back, my blood sugar I think was like 150, but my hemoglobin A_{1c} was 8 point something, and I'm like, you've got to be kidding me.

Seemingly, irrefutable laboratory results interrupted Livia's faith or belief, concerning her status with diabetes. Later, Livia again pushes back with her knowledge of the disease versus the diagnoses made based on data. The pushback is Livia's way of clarifying the facts to make intelligible or informed decisions about living with T2DM. Nevertheless, at this point, knowledge from the data frustrates her faith.

Fix

The participants with T2DM overwhelmingly focused on fixing their problems (426 codes), once understood, as found in the category of faith. Fixes resulted in almost three times more from faith than fear. Of the two causes, Fixes only reciprocated with a response to one; that is, Faith. However, fixes had two possible responses, with the overwhelming majority building the participant's faith or understanding their condition, and to a much less degree, it elicited the emotion of frustration.

Fix-to-Faith

The process of the participants with T2DM from fix-to-faith came through finding solutions, which is the same process from faith-to-fixing the problem. The only difference is the generating source.

Social Constructs

Carlos demonstrated a solution the women in the church found in managing their health in a community setting. He stated:

> The ladies actually used...this area right here on the other side of this wall used to be the dining room before we build this big dining room, so the ladies started using, a certain night of the week, they would come and do aerobics...

Carlos continued:

> One thing...that is different now is most of the time when they cook now, they try to make something for, they think about the diabetics. I think it started with the old first lady—she was diabetic, really bad...She started making people more alert about it. [She would say] You all don't want what I got here, so they started doing classes on it. Started to do stuff, cooking a different way for diabetics.

In these paragraphs, the community got involved in combating the adverse effects of health problems, especially diabetes. Livia states, "if I could implement the exercise, I probably would do better." Although she is physically unable, she believes that exercising is the solution to her problems with diabetes. In other words, based on her experiences, the ability to use the exercising facilities her church made available to the community gave her reason to believe in the possibility of managing and eliminating problems with T2DM.

Knowledge

Carlos's doctor validated his knowledge base decision to exercise and lose weight. Carlos implemented a plan to fix his problems based on information gained over the years that suggested that his array of challenges had connections to dieting and exercising. He said:

> So, the exercise and the losing of the weight fixed the blood pressure because my doctor said, when you come in for your physical, we'll monitor that. If this checks out, we'll take you off blood pressure medication.

The doctors' surprise revealed that he had given up on the belief that diet and exercise would help Carlos after years of warning. In effect, the doctor indicated that dieting and exercising was a secondary plan of issuing medication to solve problems Carlos experienced. Nevertheless, through the process of dieting and exercising Carlos found a solution that increased his faith that he could eliminate T2DM. In this case, the growth in faith experienced by Carlos, and validated by his doctor, is equivalent to self-efficacy.

Through self-directed learning, Nick eventually reached his goal of managing diabetes mellitus without medication despite his limited ability to exercise because of problems with his knees. As a result, he is a mentor greatly admired in his community. He said:

> I try to share what works for me. We just had a class…and…called and asked, if I'd come out and…could come in and talked about diabetes. So I shared with them what worked, worked for me. And I said I guarantee that if you would [do that repetitively], if you're a Type-2 Diabetic, you don't have to be on medication. You can beat it, but you have to discipline yourself, and I told them about the complex carbs. I got a whole list of them. Eat more complex carbs.

Nick demonstrates self-assured faith that others can "beat" diabetes by following his example of modifying their diet, and in so doing, they will maintain weight control and eliminate the need for T2DM medication. Therefore, Nick's self-directed learning resulted in him fixing his problems with T2DM, strengthened his faith, and gave him the confidence to help others. This self-efficacy took considerable time and effort, as he learned from the literature, mentors, and experience.

Fix-to-Frustration

A little over one-half of the participants with T2DM codes extending from the action of "fix," led to the emotion of frustration through complicated processes. In other words, complicated processes frustrated the participants. Through both social constructs and their knowledge of T2DM, they desired simple solutions or less complex solutions.

Social Constructs

Livia, who suffers from knee problems, strongly desires simple solutions in managing her T2DM. She states:

> 65 pounds and I felt real good about myself, and these years went on, and you know, the weight came back up. So, it's just kind of disheartening because everybody say do this and do that and it's not like I don't want to, but if I'm in pain, then to me it's not an option, and I just feel like I should have a quick fix, do you know what I mean? I say, now everybody else; they have these surgeries or whatever, but nobody say, well _____I'm going to sign you up, you need the surgery. No, ___ need to get out and walk 24/7, and it really gets to me because you know, I know I can, and if I make myself get out and walk, but then there is the part that say, I dont wan-a-be in pain. I don't take pain medicine; I don't take pain medicine. I've been given pain medicine, but I have a high tolerance to pain, I'd rather deal with the pain than be an addict.

Livia expresses frustration in not being able to do as others, but also from the lack of solutions for those with a handicap in managing T2DM and associated complications. She gives proof that she would exercise if able by the fact that she lost 65 pounds before her knee problems. She also feels frustration from the seeming lack of concern of doctors about the medications that she believes bombard the organs in her body with detrimental side effects. The best phrase she had to simplify the matter is "quick fix."

Knowledge

Nick demonstrates the frustration from fixes based on knowledge gained through experience. He states:

> Yeah, now you're talking 50. It started getting worse, I had to pee so much at night I would get a milk jug, and I would pee in the milk jug and go back to sleep, wake up again, pee again. I had to go dump that thing before the night was done. I was peeing that much...So then I decided well I quit taking Actos 'cause then I was, I'm skipping but it was making me fat, I quit taking Actos and the Glyburide.

Nick learned that managing T2DM could not happen with medication alone. He learned that he needed to take diabetes medication and alter his diet. Also, he learned that certain medications worked against him losing weight, thereby, complicating his management of T2DM. Therefore, through experience, Nick gained knowledge that led to frustration.

Fear

In Chapter 13, fear is thoroughly discussed in its significant role to help those with T2DM manage the disease through their social constructs. However, the number of codes (165) is a distant third behind faith and fixes in managing or eliminating T2DM (see Table 15.2). The emotion of fear had one of the three processes that produced an action or changed the participant's perception (faith) of T2DM. Fear had a unidirectional relationship between the "action" categories (fix or fatalism) and a bidirectional relationship to *the symbolic interaction* (faith) of the participant.

Fear-to-Fix

In cases where participants with T2DM experienced the emotion of fear, "fixing" the problem through the interaction of flight from the circumstance that caused the fear was three times the likely the outcome.

120   *Emerging Theory*

The interaction that bridges fear and fix is fight, and it only flowed from fear to fix the problem as opposed to becoming a victim of diabetes. Fighting the problem came through means of the participants' social constructs and their knowledge.

Social Constructs

Carlos emphatically tells what he believes COGIC diabetes sufferers in need from the social construct of their church. He said:

> And again, especially with people who have grown up in Church of God and Christ, Holiness churches, a lot of times to me, probably the better motivation tactic is the fear factor. So, maybe they start showing people look, this is what can happen to you. You can lose your limbs, lose your eyesight and kidney damage 'cause I know when I was a kid, as a matter of fact, diabetes, that was a term that came later. In fact, when I was a kid, it was sugar. I'm like, that didn't sound too bad to me, sounds pretty sweet, you know what I'm saying?

Carlos believes that preachers should use the same tactics COGIC members are accustomed to hearing to motivate them to avoid hell at all cost. That is, give them the "fear factor" concerning T2DM.

Knowledge

Carlos also demonstrates how knowledge about T2DM motivates participants to fight or resist circumstances that add to the problems of diabetes. He said:

> Now, I got scared a little bit, you know. So, I ain't going out like this, so I got serious, even though I was tired coming home from the long drive, I would come home, I'd go exercise first. We have an actual gym here in the church and so—but I made a plan.

Carlos proclaimed that a full knowledge of T2DM gained through years of seeing his family suffer from the effects of diabetes caused him to develop a plan to fight back and fix the problem.

Fear-to-Fatalism

Only 5% of the time did the participants with T2DM experience fear that led to fatalism. As seen in Chapter 13 and Figure 15.1, fear is the catalyst that elicited one of the three responses. The most prevalent was the familiar "fight or flight" processes discussed in Chapter 13.

The fear-to-fatalism process is the flight from the problem, as seen in only eight cases equally divided between social constructs and the knowledge of those with T2DM.

Social Constructs

Livia said:

> So, my fear for her is it going to really sock it to her because she won't check hers and so I just feel like if I could just get a grip. Maybe I could help all of us, you know as far as, maybe trying to be creative, but it's hard at my age, trying to be creative with a meals.

Within the social constructs of Livia, she expresses a desire to help loved ones by creating meals that those with T2DM would appreciate. Her lament indicates that despite her fear of diabetes that she passes on to family members, they flee or ignore the warnings by continually eating meals that will lead to their demise.

Knowledge

Livia said:

> The Burger King did it. It wasn't the grits because I've seen patients in the hospital, and they give grits. It's just the portion and so a lot of times, we, because we feel good or whatever. We just keep doing what we're doing, we just keep eating and keep eating the sweets and keep eating because we don't feel anything and then one thing I've seen about diabetes. When it give you that sucker punch, there ain't no returning, it can't be reversed, and that's what I see a lot with us as church people. You know, we go, and we still eat the wrong thing.

Livia expresses frustration with those whom she loves, her husband, and church members with T2DM that continued to eat unhealthy meals with the knowledge of a looming "sucker punch." Like Livia, other participants feared the worst-case scenario, but unlike Livia, some continued to eat unhealthy meals that will cause diabetes complications. The most frightening was hearing about the last days of her dad when she lamented:

> Yeah, his legs are turning dark. But he was one who decided, ate what he wanted. I'd watch my father go in the hospital with complications of diabetes. Within a month they took him off insulin and took him off pills 'cause he was eating what they told him. [Meaning, what they told him not to eat.]

Fear-to-Faith

Surprisingly, only fewer codes of those with T2DM related to the effects of fear to faith as opposed to faith to fear. Moreover, the three codes were more than 12 times less, with two concerned the social constructs and the other, the knowledge of those with T2DM. The knowledge is the same as seen in Figure 13.4 and called the precautionary action. In other words, the participants reacted to fear based on the knowledge that changes their perception (faith).

Social Constructs

In one example, Glenn stated:

> But I didn't know what diabetes was. I seen it with my grandmother and some others and stuff, they're talking about oh if you get your foot cut, don't get your foot cut if you have diabetes. Don't stub your toe. It's hard for you to heal if you get diabetes, and I'm going to tell you one thing. Before I even got diagnosed with it, if I get a little cut or bruise on me, I will try and watch it to see how fast it heals and a few times I heal real quick, and I said shoot, I'm in good shape, you know, but I haven't got cut lately where I check it out.

Glenn revealed that his primary source of knowledge about diabetes came from fragmented teaching and observation of his ancestors struggling with the effects of diabetes. Glenn's sensitization through fear caused him to monitor the healing of his injuries as an indicator of his diabetes status. In other words, if he healed normally, in his estimate, he believed he did not have diabetes, or his case was not severe.

Knowledge

Arianna shows the only case related to the knowledge that changes the participant's perception because of fear. She said:

> Well, I'm just bad about taking medicine. So I really never took that half in the morning, maybe a couple of times. So, I'm still taking the one at night.

Arianna did not believe she had diabetes, and she was afraid of medications given to those with T2DM. However, her knowledge concerning the adverse effects of T2DM on diabetic patients changed her perception (faith) and caused her to take precaution by taking a portion of the medication.

Frustration

The number of codes related to the frustration experienced by those with T2DM is slightly less but comparable to the number associated with fear. Both frustration and fear are the two emotions expressed by the participants concerning T2DM that has a similarly low number of coded processes in comparison to the total number of codes in the category (Table 15.2). However, like the "fix" category, frustration only has two processes that influence separate concepts.

Frustration-to-Fatalism

The participants with T2DM experienced frustration through processes with hegemonic overtones causing them to give up on trying doing things associated with managing T2DM. These examples are from participants who followed poor examples or felt less appreciated through hegemonic acts through the omission of statements or hegemonic statements, respectively. In either case, hegemonic processes led to fatalistic approaches to the participants' management of diabetes.

Social Constructs

Frustration-to-fatalism occurred primarily through the participants' social constructs of doctors. However, the most influential examples were from the social constructs of the church leadership, but, none of the codes related to church leadership regarding knowledge. This fact is reasonable considering education or understanding usually followed the experiences within the social construct, and the hegemony of the leaders extended from the omission of information. Moreover, a church leader corroborated this supposition when explicitly stating the same.

PREACHER'S OMISSION

Carlos reveals the hegemony of leadership based on the omission of information. He states, "You know the COGIC we'll send you to hell on almost anything, we skip that part [weight], cause the preacher is overweight." Since the participants were reverent and followed the examples of those in church leadership positions, Carlos surmised the increased obesity in the church members is reflected in them mimicking the governance behind the pulpits. According to Carlos, preachers avoid the subject of weight because it is self-reflective of said destructiveness. Therefore, through omission and hegemony, COGIC church leaders lead the members into a fatalistic approach to managing diabetes.

124   *Emerging Theory*

In several paragraphs of conversations, Carlos reveals his knowledge of preachers who through hegemonic practices hinder progress by continuing dated practices. He states:

> You've got to allow the younger generation to—because they've got fresh ideas. They've got more information at their disposal than the older generation. They getting it from the social media, they getting it from the websites; and the leadership of the church, for the most part, as you know, they've been around, they hold onto their position, I mean forever until they die.

DOCTOR'S HEGEMONY

Glenn's doctor promoted fatalism through hegemonic overtones. Glenn states:

> Cause I know when I was about 14 or 15, I went to the doctor, me and a White boy and it was like a summer job or something, we was taking a physical for or something. Even then, my blood pressure was high, and you know, I could hear him saying, most Black people got high blood pressure. It's like, it's normal for Black people to have high blood pressure anyway, like it's no big deal, like they going to have high blood pressure, but White people have it too, just as much as Black people.

The doctor made Glenn feel as though he should give up because Black people will predictably have high blood pressure. Glenn added, "They make you feel bad sometime, you know and people like that you got looking over your body, you know, putting your life in their hands." Glenn expresses his sense of frustration through hegemonic processes that pushed him toward fatalism, at least in thought, to avoid being at the mercy of the perpetrator, his doctor.

Knowledge

DOCTOR'S HEGEMONY

For reasons previously mentioned, codes revealing the frustration of the participants followed by fatalism did not come through church leadership. Only two codes appeared, and both extended from doctors. Livia stated:

> But, you know, I go to these doctors, I go to a cardiologist. I've been going to one for years because I have palpitations, which they really can't explain why I have them and I don't have them all the time, but

I do have them. So haven't had a heart attack or nothing like that, but every time I go, he's preaching to me about my weight and like I do want to lose weight, I have done it. When I first retired in 2008, I was walking, and I lost 65 pounds.

Livia is frustrated with the doctors' continual insistence that she loses weight without considering her history. She explained that her previous loss of 65 lbs, before her handicap, did not prevent the onset of diabetes. She explained, "everybody say do this and do that," which includes doctors, who are not working with her to find means of exercising with her handicap. Furthermore, they have not explained the seemingly greater problem of palpation that relates to her heart condition. She reduces the doctors' efforts to matters of "preaching," which is another way of saying hegemonic. Because of the doctors' felt insensitivity, Livia takes a fatalistic approach to manage her diabetes by making little effort to exercise.

Frustration-to-Faith

The frustration-to-faith process of those with T2DM is the same suspicion seen with the faith-to-frustration connection. The number of codes between frustration and faith is equally low at five from either direction. However, the participants are nearly five times more likely to have occurrences of frustrations leading to fatalism (24, Table 15.2) than from the frustration to a weakening of their faith (5, Table 15.2).

Social constructs

DOCTOR'S DEFICIT THINKING

Only two codes emerge related to the social constructs of the participants with diabetes. Both codes came from Glenn's data, and he said:

> One time, they did have me thinking just White people couldn't get it, diseases like diabetes and high blood pressure. Like I said, I was illiterate; you know what I'm saying? And just illiterate till not long ago really, but you know, and I hear a lot of White people saying, oh, this or that, back in the day, but now sometime I go to the doctor or whatever and White people is in there with diabetes and all that, they got it too, you know what I'm saying?

By listening, Glenn accumulated enough knowledge to refute misleading claims from doctors who gave him the impression that diabetes and other diseases were African-American diseases. Glenn admitted that his doctor's deficit thinking affected his faith for years. Therefore, for years,

126 *Emerging Theory*

Glenn blamed his ethnicity for his problem with diabetes. With uncertainty, he wondered if he had diabetes because he was not overweight, and his glucose readings were normal. As a result, Glenn could take one of the two routes to fatalism through processes of surrendering or the hegemony of his doctor, if he had not changed primary care physicians.

He expressed this belief (faith) when he said of his new doctor,

> he do set down and talk to me like you talking to me…I tell you what the doctor I got now stayed in that room with me longer the first time, longer than my other doctor did, three to four years.

The differences in Glenn's faith or belief about diabetes before and after his new doctor is evident. His questioning his status comes from years of remaining silent in the presence of a physician whose job it is to inform patients. His reluctance to ask the new doctor questions about his condition that he asked during the interview extends from at least three years of oppression due to deficit thinking.

Knowledge

Nick's overlapping paragraphs with codes from fear-to-faith in social constructs, and fear, in frustration-to-faith through the suspicion processes, yet both exist. He states:

> So I started taking that, but when I walked out of his office, I was like cholesterol. I didn't know much about it but sounds like I'd been eating too much fatty foods…So I decided well I am gonna do something different. I'm going to cut out beef and pork and stick with chicken, fish, and turkey.

The prompting word was "cholesterol," which elicited fear because of another disease but also stored knowledge that connected it to dietary intake. Notice, the doctor did not suggest a connection, but his statements made Nick suspicious or question the proposed cure. Based on his knowledge, Nick believed or had faith enough to make an informed decision in managing the new condition that further complicated his diabetes.

Fatalism

Fatalism is the last major category that emerged to explain a connecting set of data from the participants with T2DM. However, the number of codes is less than one-third (52, Table 15.2) of the closest category, frustration (159, Table 15.2, and Figure 15.1). The 52 codes of data exclusively related to fatalism divide almost evenly between the participants' social constructs and their knowledge of T2DM. Another significant difference based on the participants' data are all associated processes with a relationship to fatalism were toward fatalism, never outward. For example, from fear (8, Table 15.2), by methods of flight, from faith (32, Table 15.2), by processes of surrendering, and from frustration (24, Table 15.2), through hegemony, and none reverses or go another direction. As a result, they have no alternative to carrying out the fatalistic behavior once the process toward fatalism begins. However, it is important to note that only 45% (52, Table 15.2) of the fatalism codes came from unconnected sources, whereas between 59% and 78% of the other codes are not connected. In other words, when a person stops trying to manage their diabetes, the cause is much easier to discover, which provides hope for even the worse cases of mismanaging T2DM.

Social Constructs

Carlos shows the willingness of some COGIC members with diabetes to surrender to old eating habits despite the doctors' warning. He said:

> But the doctor done told you, you know, to stop eating sweets and stuff, but they keep doing it. To me, we just as sick as the guy that's smoking the cigarette and right on the package, it says it cause cancer. But the doctor, what are we doing? We doing the same thing.

Carlos's reference to cigarettes is an example of a killer habit repugnant to COGIC members, along with drinking alcohol, both preached against from the pulpit. At the same time, some with T2DM ignore the warning from doctors and die because they refuse to repress eating certain foods. One of Livia's statement is perhaps the best example that connects fatalism to the social constructs of the COGIC members with T2DM through the process of surrendering (see also Chapter 13, affectivity). She said, in part:

> My dad got out of the hospital; he said God had gave him all the years that he promised. He was going to eat what he wanted, and he did just that. My dad didn't have bad hemoglobin A_{1c}, so what gives with that?

Livia's dad expressed satisfaction with the length of time he lived, took the fatalistic approach of ignoring all dietary precautions, and enjoyed the remainder of his life. Livia gave the impression that she admired the stance that he took and seemed to entertain the idea for her future. The concept is likely since she thought the doctors made an incorrect diagnosis of her dad's condition and questioned the doctor's diagnosis of her having diabetes. Additionally, she has a physical handicap that prevents her from exercising. Therefore, the accumulation of frustrations that affect her faith or belief about her T2DM status could conceivably result in her fatalistically surrendering like her dad.

Knowledge

Nick gave the example of a COGIC member with diabetes who took a fatalistic approach to manage his diabetes. He said, "Yeah, he'd get out of the hospital, continuing to eat like he was, he'd revert back to what he was doing, he's back on insulin, back on pills and ultimately it took him out." Despite his dad's knowledge of the consequences, if, for no other reason than his experience, he elected to continue with his destructive eating habits until his death.

Finally, the dissecting of the core category, substantive living, although thorough, are presented in simplified relationships between categories in terms of their actions, interactions, emotions, as they relate to the participants' social constructs and knowledge. However, realistically, the transcribed paragraphs usually presented complicated conundrums that resulted in chain reactions, while maintaining an air of familiarity. For example, a poor solution in the doctor's choice of medicines added to Nick's mistrust of T2DM medication. Therefore, the discovered processes of learning, the fix, medication, caused a change in perception, faith, concerning proper T2DM management. The change in perception resulted from sensitization processes in the faith-to-fear axiom, which caused mistrust in the medication, and fear spun off into two directions and for good reasons. First, the mistrust initiated the fear-to-fatalism reaction driven by a flight response that resulted in discontinuing the medication that caused weight gain, which worsens diabetes. On the other hand, the achievement of self-efficacy in the fix-to-faith axiom caused faith to channeled fear back to fix (fear-to-fix axiom) using fight as the interaction to find another solution.

16 Substantive Living

The overarching theoretical explanation binding the discovered categories of those with type 2 diabetes mellitus (T2DM) through codes, memos, and diagrams is their quest for substantive living (SL) which made up the parts as dissected in Chapter 15. Through careful inductive analysis, categories emerged, but it took deductive analysis by rethinking schematics and data to discover the goals of the participants and the mentors that influence their decision concerning T2DM. The abstraction of the data revealed that the primary objective of the participants is to live a substantive life. As defined earlier, "Substantive Living, the core category, is the participants' goal of having and doing the things they enjoyed after years of cultivating those behaviors." COGIC church members live highly structured and restricted lives but relish the customs of their heritage. Many of these customs included popular ethnic foods for enjoyment in private and social settings. Type 2 diabetes mellitus (T2DM) interrupts these customs, and every decision made by the participants reflects their desire to live meaningful lives, which are lives close to their norms.

Nevertheless, the abstraction of the core category necessitated a continual abstract view of the diagrams and memos developed from the participants' data. The evolution of the encompassing matrix of Figure 15.1 produced two unplanned visual effects. The first is the formation of a cross in the middle with faith connecting to the other major concepts. Though surprising, it seemed fitting for the subculture of African-Americans with T2DM in the COGIC church. Most surprising is the pyramid that emerged after considering the familiar look of the matrix in Figure 15.1, derived from the participants' data. That is, considering the prominence of faith because of its significantly greater number of codes elicited the thought of elevating it above the others. From a bird's-eye view, this restructuring produced the startling awareness that a pyramid has the shape of the cross in the middle. Furthermore, the resulting three-dimensional model in Figure 16.1 of a pyramid better illustrates and simplifies a complex theory of how the COGIC subculture of African-Americans with T2DM integrate faith, knowledge, and social constructs. The elevation of faith

130 *Emerging Theory*

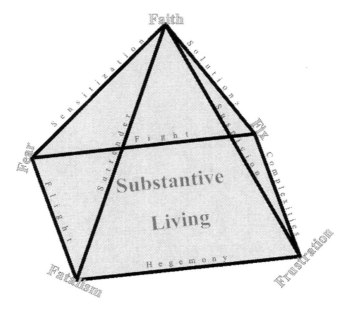

Figure 16.1 Afro-Theistic Theory in 3D.

mimics not only its greater percentage of codes but also the difficulty of other categories in affecting changes in it.

Conversely, the participants' faith could easily affect changes in the others. In other words, based on the participants' statistics in Table 15.2, change is more probable when going downhill as opposed to uphill. However, there is one exception; there are more fix-to-faith (uphill) codes than faith-to-fix (downhill). The increased numbers reflect the significantly greater number of codes for Nick and Carlos in the "fix" category of Table 15.2, while the other three participants had a larger number in the "faith" concept. Intriguingly, although slightly less, the number of codes for Nick and Carlos (see Table 15.2) in the faith category were comparable to the other participants. Therefore, the primary source of the increased numbers in the "fix" category for these two are the results of amplified efforts to fix their problems with T2DM. Their data reflects this finding since the fix-to-faith route obtained by the process of finding solutions took years of knowledge gained through literature, mentors, and experience. However, they became the only two whose data rewards them with the self-efficacy status. Conceptually the difficulty in achieving self-efficacy reflects the difficulties of the average American to climb the Pyramid Khafre in Egypt. For most, it would take years of changing habits to save the monies to afford the trip, obtain permission, overcome fears of heights, and become physically fit.

Additionally, a look at the total number of codes in each category (see Table 15.2) reflects the participants' efforts to fix their problem, mainly because of Nick and Carlos, and ranks second to that of faith. Therefore, theoretically, the proactive action of the category "fix" rightfully belong to the North, and the reactive response of frustration, with the fewest number of codes, is in the South. On the other hand, the evenly plain categories of fear, fix, frustration, and fatalism permits a more fluid lateral movement between the concepts and therefore, more quickly changed, corresponds with the participants' data. Finally, along the edges are the connecting processes that enclose the pyramid and captures the space that defines substantive living (SL).

As seen in Table 15.2, 281 of the 318 SL codes directly connects to the five categories of faith, fix, fear, frustration, and fatalism, previously discussed. Only a small percentage of the codes (37) had an exclusive relationship to the overarching SL category, as opposed to most of the others to their respective five classifications. One example of SL in isolation is with Glenn's father. He said:

> No, he was diagnosed when he got sick, right before he died. Everything, he had diabetes right before he died, everything—when he first got sick, he got burned with some hot water. Then everything started.

Here, Glenn's dad lived carefully not to incur injuries while he continued eating the tasty foods that he enjoyed. Rather than stop eating the foods that he desired, he trusted the myth that diabetes only affected those who were carelessly injured. Glenn learned this myth from his grandmother, which caused him to monitor the healing of any injuries to his body obsessively.

SL and Faith

Nearly 98% of the SL codes linked to one of the five substantiated categories, connected to faith. Therefore, the participants' faith, or what they believed about T2DM, for all practical purposes, is SL. Although the terms are practically synonymous, SL slightly differs because it reflects the participants' actions based upon their belief. It usually meant that the participants continued eating the types of foods they enjoyed. For example, Nick said:

> So I would go there drinking 'cause I was just always thirsty. Didn't know I was doing but I was getting the Slurpee's. I'd go get the orange slurp. It was always my favorite flavor.

132 *Emerging Theory*

Before Nick emerged with self-efficacy, he had to break his habit of taking advantage of the fringe benefits from his job. The sweet drinks became habit-forming like drugs, perhaps due to the lack of planned moderation. In either case, SL related to faith explains the participants' desires to continue eating as though T2DM did not exist. It explains Livia and Nick's dad refusal to modify their diet because of a desire to continue eating the foods they enjoyed. Finally, it tells Livia's husband, who enjoyed her cooking, and others who desired things to stay as they were before a diagnosis of T2DM.

SL and Fix

Nick gives the only code directly connecting SL to fix. He stated:

> I get, you don't get tired of eating those meals? No, I don't, 'cause I want to live. You can go from oatmeal; Cheerios to both got oats still got the same effect. I decided I wanted to live. So here it is now, I wake up this morning I take my blood sugar, 82. I still take the Glucophage 'cause she told me to. My next time, they said, already told me... It's coming up; she's going to say if you keep doing what you're doing you'll get off of this.

Through self-directed learning, Nick adjusted his desire for foods that he loves to foods that were healthy and sustainable. While others wondered if he got tired of the same meals, he merely demonstrated how to vary the meals to continue to enjoy them. After observing Nick in different settings, even at the church feasts, he always selected healthy and satisfying foods in modest portions.

SL and Fear

Nick also gave the only case that connected SL and fear. He said:

> I would drink one and a couple hours later I was so thirsty again, go back and drink another one. I was like I can't stay awake. Sometimes I have to go park somewhere I know no ones at, just to try to take a nap. Try to wake up and pretty much the same thing again. Then in church, I started noticing when I really, man this is wrong, something wrong. I would see people's silhouette, but I couldn't see their mouth moving or their eyes, it affected my vision.

Nick relates the consequences of him ignoring his diagnosis of T2DM for the sake of SL to continue the foods he loved. That is, until uncontrolled diabetes produced fear and fear produces action, as seen in Figure 13.4.

SL and Frustration

Livia gave the only example of connecting frustration to SL. She said:

> I really want to come off it, and I know, I believe that weight got a lot—I'm hoping that if I get off the weight, then maybe I can get rid of the medicine. I'm just really hoping.

Livia's frustration is evident, but making the connection to SL is more subtle. Livia is wrestling with the means of losing weight because she can no longer exercise as she did to lose 65 pounds. Nick has the same problems with his knees and still manages to keep his T2DM under control. Further, the difference is that Nick modified his diet, and Livia has not. Meaning, her desire for SL, which usually means eating accustomed meals, according to data, has not changed significantly enough.

SL and Fatalism

Three incidences gave codes connecting SL and fatalism. Nick stated, "She tried to teach me, but you know being young like I was, it was really going in one ear, out the other." In this example, Nick explained that his youth interfered with his better judgment of listening to his doctor and modifying his diet to manage his diabetes. Therefore, SL or the desire to continue with eating rituals that brought acquired pleasure took precedence over seemingly distant problems.

Summary of Findings

This study began by creating an open atmosphere and establishing rapport with the participants. After immersion in the collected data, it revealed five primary categories: faith, fix, fear, frustration, and fatalism. Through inductive and deductive processes of parsed coding and memo writing evolve the diagrams and tables used to develop a theory grounded in the collected data. The resulting theory grounded in data explained how faith, knowledge, and the social constructs of the COGIC members with T2DM work together in managing the disease. The saturation of the categories came from tens to hundreds of codes whose decreasing numbers helped rank their significance. The processes connecting the concepts resulted from the social constructs or self-directed learning of the participants.

The multiple examples from the five participants and examined through theoretical sampling validated the findings. Additionally, through abstraction of the data emerged the core category, Substantive Living (SL), which necessarily revealed an overarching purpose of the five categories established by the participants' data. The unexpected visual effects of

134 *Emerging Theory*

Figure 15.1 and then Figure 16.1 significantly help to conceptualize the findings in the form of a theory. In so doing, they established faith as the participants' primary category and its close relationship to SL as their purpose in living with T2DM. Table 15.2 gives the invaluable statistics of the categories and their connecting processes. Although the codes for each outnumbered their processes or actions that connected them, their statistics prove indispensable to understanding the five concepts.

A significantly greater number of codes for faith helped the abstraction to elevate it above the others, which symbolize the difficulty for other categories to affect it, but the ease by which it affected the others. Furthermore, the North and South polarity of the proactive action of the fix concept versus the reactive act of fatalism, which is less in number, corresponds to the greater efforts to live and not die with diabetes. The surprisingly more considerable number of codes corresponding to the processes of the fix-to-faith interactions over the faith-to-fix interactions signifies the means (*desire* to fix) and difficulty (*uphill*) of achieving *self-efficacy*.

The East and West axis, with a similar number of codes, corresponds to the categorical emotions of frustration and fear. Overall, the participants exhibited the emotion of fear slightly more, but comparable to frustration. When taking action, fear usually resulted in the participants fighting to fix their problems to live, and much less in fleeing to a fatalistic death. On the other hand, frustrated participants were three times more likely to resort to fatalism than when they feared. Surprisingly, they *equally* resorted to fix or fatalism, respectively. Comparatively, they rarely affected faith, again proof of the difficulty in effecting change uphill (Table 15.2).

Also remarkable was that by combining the participants' relatively lower number of processes or actions formed four quadrants that had an unequal, in number, but the opposite effect to their respective categorical quadrants (Table 15.1). The contradicting activities seem to balance the participants' status and reveal the complexities of their diabetes management. Interestingly, according to the statistics in Table 15.2, the accumulation of codes in each category far exceeded those departing, but fatalism had no exit. The accumulation means that to some extent, the participants necessarily harbored aspects of each of the five categories at any given time since they exceeded the number exiting. Finally, the fact that the Fatalism category does not have an exit seems significant relative to efforts to continue living. The concluding Part 6 finalizes the study with the findings, implications, and most importantly, the resulting permeated learning theory and its future research potentials.

Part 6
The Theory
Permeated Learning Emergence

Part 6 wraps up this study with the complete development of the theory of permeated learning (PL) with substantive living as the orchestrating core factor at the root of all actions, interactions, and emotions. Chapter 17 begins the completion of the theory by examining the key findings. In so doing, the chapter revisits the research questions and summarizes the findings, which gives answers to the inquiries. Chapter 18 is devoted totally to completing the theory development of permeated learning theory in relationship to substantive living. Chapter 19 continues with the implications and recommendations of the resulting PL theory. Chapter 20 is a superimposing connection of the PL theory to the diaspora and pro-slavery Afro-Theism. Finally, Chapter 21 concludes by bridging the gap in the literature and the application of the PL theory.

17 Key Finding

This study purposed to develop a theory grounded in the data of the way adult African-American COGIC members with type 2 diabetes mellitus (T2DM) construct their understanding that reconciled their faith with their knowledge of diabetes. The development of theory required a threefold examination of the subculture to answer four research questions. That is, (1) it required the determination of the COGIC members' faith concerning diabetes, (2) their knowledge of T2DM, and (3) the relationship of both to their social constructs.

There emerged several important findings relevant to the COGIC members with T2DM, but also for the African-American community with diabetes. Additionally, the results of this study are beneficial for the diabetic community as a whole. The study also revealed significant findings that contradicted several held views concerning this group's faith, knowledge, and social constructs based upon the research questions.

Faith

Defining faith in connection to COGIC participants with T2DM from their perspective proves to be more of a conundrum than it was first believed to be possible. Although they openly expressed a belief in God based on their Afro-Theistic cultural practice, as predicted by Eltis (2008), the participants did not connect their faith in God with diabetes. Instead, they kept faith in God separated from their beliefs about diabetes. Therefore, the participants kept an open mind to the realities of oppositions. For example, they acknowledged the hegemonic activities of doctors and pastors concerning matters of diabetes. Their compartmentalized faith gave the participants independence when responding to social injustices.

Therefore, the religious practices of these individuals do not make them predictable in the choices they make during a crisis. Their ability to compartmentalize their belief means they could be the pacifists despised by Asante (1988), or support critical race theorists like Giles (2010). For the COGIC member with diabetes in this study, beliefs concerning social issues about the disease did not vary based upon economic status, as predicted by Hurston (1981). The ability to compartmentalize their faith explains the diversity in the church during the civil rights movement in the 1960s. Some, like the researcher's dad, became pacifists, others supported the church leaders' decision to support Martin Luther King (see COGIC History), and yet others empathized and held Malcolm X's funeral in their church. Furthermore, COGIC members' faith allowed them to switch positions during other crises. For example, the researcher's dad, a church elder, became an activist to marry an interracial couple at an unacceptable time in the South, in the 1960s.

A composite definition of the participants' compartmentalized faith proved crucial to this study. Despite the compartmentalizing of their faith, the five participants' definition overlapped and coalesced into only three parts. They believe that COGIC members with diabetes should respond with knowledge based upon their beliefs about the disease while relying on God for circumstances beyond their control. The participants did not necessarily accept the clinician's diagnosis of their condition but gathered information from various sources to determine the degree of severity and then acted according to that belief.

Knowledge

The participants obtained knowledge from diverse sources but relied heavily upon the understanding of T2DM learned from ancestral past and current family members' experiences. These served as *mentors*, and in a secondary sense, so did doctors, pastors, celebrities, and knowledgeable individuals, whom the participants made comparisons to their condition. Regardless of the source of knowledge, it did not always result in action from the participants. It took the ingredient of fear to move the participants to one of three decisions. Through different degrees, they either worked to fix (most frequent) their problems with T2DM based on their comparisons, continued fatalistic eating habits, or pursued self-directed learning (least frequent) opportunities.

During times of self-directed learning, the participants only use literature to confirm or dispute a diagnosis or enhance their knowledge about a product that others used to mitigate the effects of diabetes. Interestingly, the belief (faith-to-fear, Table 15.2) of these individuals concerning their status with T2DM had more than 12 times the influence on fear (fear-to-faith, Table 15.2) than the low response to fear for self-directed learning. Therefore, the knowledge gained through the experiences of mentors heavily influenced their beliefs or faith and caused greater fear of diabetes than the literature's impact on their faith. None of the participants attempted to learn about diabetes before their diagnosis. The younger the participant during the time of the doctors' warning, the least likely they would respond by learning or attempting to prevent the disease.

Conversely, the longer periods of warning produced the most avid efforts to manage T2DM, provided that they believe (faith) the diagnosis.

For example, both Carlos and Nick became self-directed learners and obtained a high degree of self-efficacy. However, only Carlos's faith (belief) that he had the same disease as his ancestors caused enough "fear-to-fix" the problem. Nick, on the other hand, did not attempt to "fix" this issue even though suffering from multiple complications from diabetes. It took several bouts with the disease to convince him that he had the disease of his ancestors. Once convinced, his fear propelled him into superseding Carlos in managing the disease.

Nick especially fulfilled Bandura's (1977, p. 191) "four principal sources of information: performance accomplishments, vicarious experience, verbal persuasion, and physiological states" for self-efficacy. The difference between Carlos and Nick and the others rests in Mezirow's (1997) statement that "Frames of reference are the structures of assumptions through which we understand our experiences." Overall, the other three, diagnosed later in life as having diabetes, minimally manage the disease. Again, the best explanation for the differences is Mezirow's theorized transformational learning processes of frames of references. However, these frames of references were unpredictable but depended on the individuals' faith, or belief concerning the severity of their condition by primarily making comparisons to ancestors, which fell short of knowing how the participants were learning. In the meantime, in confirmation of Baumgartner's (2011) meta-analysis concerning the application of knowledge, regardless of age, the participants acted according to their belief about T2DM based on knowledge obtained vicariously through the experiences of them with close social ties.

Social Constructs

The social constructs of the COGIC participants with T2DM proved to be the most used factor in managing diabetes based on the recorded data. The participants revealed three groups that affected their decision-making processes concerning T2DM. The social constructs consisted of primary and secondary mentors, with ancestors and family members being the primary ones, which agrees with Weiler's (2007) finding, and doctors, pastors, and others being secondary. The difference is that the participants learned from the primary mentors throughout their life before having diabetes. However, of the two in the main group, the participants mostly acted according to what they vicariously learned from ancestors, such as parents and grandparents. Finally, a tertiary group of some doctors and pastors (leaders) had an undesirable impact on them managing T2DM.

As the term social constructs suggest a psychosocial (Dewey, 1982) interaction for meaning-making, it gives the definition of constructivism substantiated by societal influences of the COGIC members. While teasing out the data of the participants, as a constructivist, and knowing the influence of the social interactions of the COGIC church from its beginning, it gave the researcher the confidence that the theory would have support from the data. However, the degree of meaning-making through these COGIC social constructs is a complete surprise. The data revealed that the participants acted based on their individualized faith concerning their diabetes status. Nonetheless, their understanding of the degree of severity (meaning-making) came through comparisons made with mentors who had the disease.

Moreover, none of the participants took action to prevent the disease regardless of the number of warnings, which correlates with their mentors. Furthermore, the participants had preconceived notions of how diabetes would appear based on what they saw in their mentors. As a result, the degree of belief varied when the physicians said they had diabetes.

For example, despite years of warning, followed by severe physical ailments from uncontrolled diabetes, Nick still did not believe he had diabetes for two reasons. First, he had spent years convinced that he was invincible, which correlated with none of his mentors having diabetes at a young age. Second, he dismissed the doctor's diagnosis after making comparisons to mentors, down to minute details, until finding the slightest of differences. Both Livia and Glenn currently live in doubt about their diagnosis, for similar and different reasons. Similarly, neither has symptoms, but both were diagnosed based on having an elevated hemoglobin A_{1c}.

They differ in their knowledge of the disease, and both the greater and lesser knowledge makes them skeptical. Furthermore, they continue to make comparisons to their ancestors. Livia's dad dismissed his doctor's diagnosis because of his age, and Glenn relied on his grandmother's bits of information about diabetes. However, both to varying degrees take precautionary actions by following their doctor's advice. Arianna ignores her doctor's advice for the most part, because she does not have symptoms of her ancestors, and her glucose readings are within normal ranges the few times that she took it. On the other hand, the diagnoses of diabetes struck fear in Carlos because of his stored memory of ancestors with diabetes, which caused him to take immediate actions to control the disease. Nevertheless, a theory grounded in the participants' data of how faith, knowledge, and social constructs works together emerged from the research questions.

Research Questions Answered

Research Question 1

What does diabetes education look like for the Afro-Theistic COGIC diabetes mellitus sufferers?

The primary source of the participants' knowledge about T2DM came through social constructs consisting of ancestors, beginning with parents and grandparents, followed by other family members. The participants' vicarious estimates defined their beliefs or faith concerning their diabetes status once diagnosed. Furthermore, this belief dictated the actions taken by the participants to manage or eradicate diabetes.

Research Question 2

How can Afro-Theistic faith and diabetes education coexist to help type 2 diabetes mellitus (T2DM) sufferers?

Answering this question required defining faith regarding diabetes since the participants compartmentalize faith based upon the point of application. Meaning, the definition of faith when applied to unseen spiritual matters is different from the participants' definition when applied to physical issues. A composite definition is the participants' belief that COGIC members with T2DM should "respond with knowledge based on their convictions about the disease while relying on God for circumstances beyond their control." To quote Carlos, "faith is one thing but man, don't be stupid." Therefore, the participants found the idea of divine healing by faith to be obtuse and repugnant.

Research Question 3

What are diabetic COGIC members' Afro-Theistic social constructs' beliefs about diabetes mellitus?

- What are the Afro-Theistic social constructs?

The social constructs of the COGIC members with T2DM consist of promoters and distractors of healthy living with the disease. The promoters of healthy lifestyles appeared in the form of mentors. Ancestors and family members served as primary sources for knowledge about T2DM, and doctors, pastors, church members, and other knowledgeable people were secondary sources. However, only primary sources serve to educate the participants concerning diabetes before the onset of the condition. In other words, the participants primarily defined diabetes as relating to their estimate of their ancestors' experiences with the disease. They learn through constructivism, which meant the meaning-making equated to individualistically constructed impressions rather than explicit teaching. As a result, the participants' belief that they did or did not have diabetes came from reflections upon ancestral experiences with the disease over a doctor's diagnosis. The distractors to healthy living came from hegemonic overtones of physicians, the omission of teachings against obesity from pastors, and the dominance of unhealthy foods during social gatherings.

Research Question 4

How does the Afro-Theistic social constructs' interpretation of diabetes mellitus overtly or covertly influence COGIC member's resolve to disregard intervention?

The answer to this question is subtle but appears to result from respect for constructivism. That is, each COGIC member with T2DM constructs knowledge and makes decisions based on their idea of "substantive living." Therefore, members of their Afro-Theistic social constructs respect the sufferer's decisions as being resolute and refrain from interference. The fact is observers seem to view these decisions as being noble, which becomes part of their folklore. For example, in admiration, Livia said, "My dad got out of the hospital; he said God had gave him all the years that he promised. He was going to eat what he wanted, and he did just that." Even when condemning these decisions, it is with reverence. For example, Nick said of his dad, "But when I walked out, I was like you know I saw my dad die from complications of diabetes." Later, Nick said, "And the whole while my dad would say you're digging your grave one fork at a time." Through this thorough investigation emerged the permeated learning theory with substantive living as a motivator, from the participants' data discussed in the next chapter.

18 Permeated Learning

The question remaining is, "What best captures the messiness in learning of these participants?" Shall we violate all that adult education theorists claim concerning adults as learners and say they are not learning. The researcher begs to differ. While not disagreeing that the learning is atypical of what academia would like to call learning, these are thinking adults, and it takes lifelong learning to reach their age. Therefore, it is incumbent for academia to make the adjustments and "figure it out" concerning the common man and woman, to keep Knowles et al.'s (2011) democratic process intact, which this research intended to do. This brief but necessary chapter reveals the theory that emerged from the connecting core and anchoring category of "substantive living," and finally answers the question concerning the type of adult learning these participants are experiencing and presents the model of learning in three dimensions. The theory captures the breadth of learning that includes the participants' faith, knowledge, and social constructs concerning T2DM that produced the actions, interactions, and emotions as the participants defined or redefined their quest for a substantive life. Finally, through further abductive reasoning to determine the meaning-making of the participants arose the permeated learning theory.

Prevailing were the participants' knowledge-based beliefs, called "faith," concerning their status with diabetes. Behind "faith" came the attempts to eradicate their condition in the knowledge-based action called "fix." The third and fourth categories were closely related to the number of codes but distant from the first two. These were the knowledge-based emotions of "fear," followed by "frustration." At a further distance in numbers is the final category, "fatalism," which is the second action taken, but in polar opposition to "fix."

Notably, there is a special group in the "flight" category, that is, an interaction following the emotion of "fear." When related to those who died, they are included in the line linking them to "fatalism" and is a summation, rather than a direct correlation. Those dying did not code to either an emotion, such as anger, or a deliberate action, like denial, yet the results were "fatalistic," in that eventually came uncontrolled diabetes and ultimately death. Although the prospect should have caused "fear," it did not, and although it seemed their "faith" lapsed into "fatalism," it did not. In fact, at this point, these individuals were resolute and unwavering in their decision. So what was this? No doubt, this is Kübler-Ross's (1970) fifth stage of death and dying designated acceptance. If they went through the other four stages, it seemed instantaneous from the purported observations. Therefore, based on others' observations of them, martyrdom seems the best description for these regal individuals who accepted the inevitable, memorialized by the multiple crosses throughout the 3D model (Figure 18.1) made of permeateted learning and anchored by substantive living. Individuals at this point seem identical to the mothers labeled as martyrs in Chapter 1. One caveat concerning martyrdom; other than Grannie Reen, the information did not come from the researcher's direct observation but seems plausible.

Nevertheless, all concepts emerged from the knowledge gained through the interactions with social constructs and produced the overarching concept called "substantive living" that anchors the "permeated learning" cross and identified the participants' purpose in all they did concerning T2DM, through the differences in the number of codes and connecting interactions of each category emerged an astonishing 3D model in the shape of a pyramid. The abstracted matrix revealed that the participants' "faith" is the primary influence of the other four categories and is strikingly similar to prevalence and importance to Cordova's (2011) "spirituality" in her study. However, the prevailing interactions from "fix-to-faith" in solving problems with T2DM revealed the difficulty of achieving self-efficacy. The small number of "fatalistic" responses correlate to the desire of participants to live. However, the connection of all concepts to "substantive living" reveals a supreme desire to enjoy or celebrate while continuing to live with accustomed cultural events, private or social, that usually involved ethnic foods, despite having diabetes.

Hence, here is a concise definition and the most helpful aspects of the permeated learning theory to encourage those with managing their diabetes and others working with them. Permeated learning is the messiness (**chaos**) in learning that results in change as knowledge slowly penetrates the very being of existence, with substantive living, providing motivation. Permeated learning, therefore, anticipates the process of personal successes and failures with a model to help focus learning towards the desired outcome. The process includes two actions (fix and fatalism), two emotions (fear and frustration), the control center (**the mind**), in charge of faith, or the belief of an individual, and the interactions between each. Self-efficacy is the process of connecting fix and faith through solutions. No solution is permanent, but maintainable, by monitoring self through the application of the permeated learning model.

Permeated Learning versus Transformational Learning

From the researcher's perspective, the word and idea of Mezirow's transformational learning relates to the text in the Greek New Testament, Romans Chapter 12 and Verse 1 (12:1), "...but be transformed by the renewal of your mind" (*The Holy Bible: English Standard Version, Containing the Old and New Testaments (ESV)*, 2011). Here, the word for transformation in Greek is the word μεταμορφόω (*met-am-or-fŏ´-o*), written as a *verb*, present, passive, imperative, second person, and plural. In other words, transformation is an ongoing action the author requested from the audience. However, the question is, what caused the action, transformation? The answer follows in the same Romans 12:1, from the *noun*, renewal, the Greek word ἀνακαινώσει (*an-ak-ah´ee-no-si*), in the dative, singular, and feminine as instructions to individuals on how to change. The word consists of two words, "*ana*" (Summers, 1995), which means *with* and the word "*kainos*" (*Exegetical Dictionary of the New Testament, V 1: Aarōn-Henōch*, 1990), which means *new*. Which gives the idea that new information or knowledge must "penetrate" the mind before transformation takes place.

In that vein, although this study did not focus on transformational learning, there are clear implications for change, but without the established standards of transformation. Because the knowledge-based experiences of the participants are fragile psychosocial (Dewey, 1982) processes, it perpetually makes their responses chaotic in direction, replete with relapses and vacillations, which makes transformation seem like the "carrot dangling before the horse." A 3D pyramid model (Figure 18.1) conceptualized the magnitude of these chaotic processes of knowledge, and the word "permeated" better captures the phenomenon of change in learning. The word permeate is most similar to the saying that "if an attitude or feeling permeates something, you can feel or see its influence clearly in every part of that thing" (Bullon et al., 2007). The difference is that the attitude or feeling are self-reflections that permeates self. Therefore, permeated learning, when considering the fluctuating attitudes, and feelings in conjunction with permeation, captures the learning experienced especially by Nick and Carlos who achieved the status of self-efficacy in their quest for substantive living. It appears that the participants changed over time as knowledge slowly permeated their mind, and very being or soul. Therefore, "permeated learning" seems to be the best explanation of the self-efficacy expressed by Nick and Carlos.

The circumstances that evoked fear is a disorienting dilemma necessary for transformation (Mezirow, 1991). Nevertheless, the actual changes were complicated and sometimes circular or repetitive, often due to the subtle nature of T2DM. Change required time, trial and error, failure, relapses, and reflection, as the slow movement toward a new

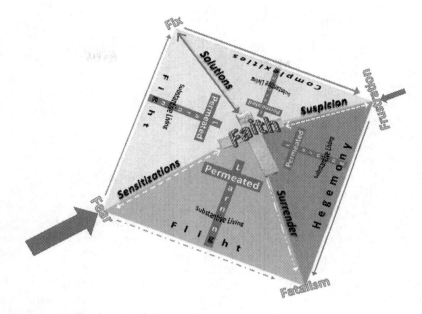

Figure 18.1 Permeated Learning Theory.

reality of healthy living permeated Nick and Carlo's mind, body, and soul, always with the threat of collapse, yet captured in the safety net of the substantive living core category. Safety net, here, is not a metaphor, neither is it necessarily safe, rather it is the reality that these individuals resorted to what they called living, as long as they could, when all else failed. Again, the problem with making this statement is the seeming permanence of transformation that disregards the reality. Namely, those with T2DM did not ride off into the sunset of success; they face daily battles that are often lost. The difference now is the resulting map to understanding the processes (actions, interactions, and emotions) that the substantive living core category captures and the permeated learning theory explains. This knowledge is useful in reducing the sense of futility with each failure.

By knowing that failure is continually part of the process of change, but having a model to identify what went wrong, and the processes to change toward the desired effect. One may set realistic goals to successfully manage, reverse the effects of, or help others prevent diabetes altogether. With this new descriptive theory comes the responsibility of using it to effect change in the diabetes status of individuals. Effecting change begins by considering the implications of the permeated learning theory, motivation of substantive living, and taking the recommended actions discussed in the following chapter.

19 Permeated Learning
Implications and Recommendations

The findings of this study have significant implications and recommendations that need to become part of the conversation in adult education, and research, to aid in its ultimate purpose of reducing diabetes in the African-American culture to one in three by the year 2050. The key is having access to the findings, and this book hopes to get the conversation started with educators. Concerning research, there are opportunities to make the results of this study available to clinicians, health professionals, and diabetes educators to initiate discussions toward change. Also, to help facilitators associated with African-American T2DM sufferers through conference presentations, peer-reviewed journal articles, and through professional development implement the permeated learning theory and substantive living motivation as a means of understanding and helping to encourage people living with diabetes to persevere. On the national stage, the Adult Education Research Conference (AERC) hosts an annual African Diaspora preconference for which this study should have representation. Locally, the Texas Association of Black Personnel in Higher Education (TABPHE) in Austin, Texas, hosts an annual conference with space to present the findings of this study. This researcher contacted the American Diabetes Association (ADA) concerning a publication in its journal or its affiliates, such as the National Institutes of Health (NIH). These widely distributed journals concerning diabetes are sure to stimulate discussions concerning African-Americans and type 2 diabetes mellitus (T2DM). Once a year, the Texas Society of Allied Health Professions (TSAHP) sponsors a professional development workshop with opportunities for presentation or a poster. These initial efforts should lead to other opportunities to expose academia to the permeated learning theory and substantive living model for assessment and management of T2DM in African-Americans.

One of the most important findings in permeated learning theory is the significant role doctors, and COGIC leaders play helping African-Americans COGIC members avoid or manage diabetes. However, those with diabetes become the mentors that the next generation emulates. All are mentors at times and hegemonic on other occasions. For example, when doctors condescendingly predict failure to African-Americans in the COGIC church, it is hegemonic. When obese pastors are not open about the relationship of obesity to diabetes, they leave space for the congregation to follow, which is hegemony through omission of helpful information. When those with diabetes in the African-Americans COGIC church do not help the youth in avoiding the same by teaching and being open, it is hegemonic by influence. Therefore, to facilitate permeated learning by substantive living from uncontrolled diabetes to management of the disease, pastors should encourage monthly meetings concerning parishioners' health, with T2DM as part of every session. Doctors of patients with T2DM should encourage them by actively seeking a list of local churches that provide the support group for African-Americans with T2DM. Personally, the study brought about a change in attitude about exercise, by doing "old folk," calisthenics daily, only taking about 15 minutes. The new approach and calisthenics are works in progress that reflect permeated learning while maintaining substantive living in managing T2DM.

Recommendations

The overall aim of the recommendations is threefold. (1) Rescue the African-American youth from current trends of diabetes in the African-American community. (2) Assist current African-Americans with diabetes to manage their disease. (3) Change the attitude of the two leading communities, medical and church, concern in African-Americans with diabetes.

The study shows that the participants in the subculture of African-Americans with T2DM rely on experiences of ancestors to determine their status despite the diagnosis of their doctor. Therefore, the recommendation suggested by one participant is advisable. That is, Carlos suggested training the youth in the COGIC church because they will influence the future. The following is that conversation:

CARLOS: But to answer your first question, I don't think—probably not as far as most of the time in our church. In the Church of God and Christ, you got big megachurches, but for the most part, you got the real small churches. Education levels are different and so, most of the time, we kind of key on moral issues and probably it's going to continue to be like that until we make room for some of the younger generation.
RESEARCHER: So what do you think that the younger generation will bring to the table? Or what do you think can change if we push in that avenue; push. What should be changed?
CARLOS: You've got to allow the younger generation to [have space] because they've got fresh ideas. They've got more information at their disposal than the older generation.

RESEARCHER: Such as what? Where are they getting this information?
CARLOS: They getting it from the social media, they getting it from the websites and the leadership of the church. For the most part, as you know, they've been around, they hold onto their position, I mean forever until they die.
RESEARCHER: Right.
CARLOS: So, we're talking generations of no change, same concepts. Same everything, but you got to make room for the younger generation, and I believe when we do that, and we kind of doing that here at this church. I know in the different auxiliaries, we don't just teach the lessons. We make room; sometime we'll have a night or whatever is promoted. Publicized in the community that maybe help professionals [are] going to be here, and they [are] going to be talking about that and I believe churches need to start doing that.
RESEARCHER: Ah-ha.

What should the youth learn? The findings of this study suggest that the place to start training young people in African-American churches is their role in diabetes management. That is, to understand the significance of them having the primary influence on the next generation. Therefore, the need exists for a proper understanding of diabetes and its effects on African-Americans. Just as important is training in churches; the study suggests that support groups in African-American churches be formed using African-Americans who are successfully managing their diabetes as facilitators.

Additionally, leaders in the medical and church community should reconsider their position in helping African-Americans control their diabetes based on the findings from this study. That is, doctors should know that African-Americans view them as prophets of doom. Therefore, along with making predictions, clinicians should immediately encourage appointments for regimented diet and exercise training, with follow-ups, when African-Americans are in the prediabetic stage. The idea is that the patient learns to prevent the onset of diabetes or to manage it if unavoidable. This mindset should also have precedence in the ADA for African-Americans to decrease the number of cases in this population. Based on this study, the medical community should actively support African-American support groups with African-American who are successfully managing their diabetes.

Pastors and leaders in the COGIC church and African-American churches, in general, should understand their role in helping African-Americans manage diabetes. That is, based on this study, members mimic them. Therefore, if the leaders do not address issues with obesity, a contributing factor to diabetes, the possibility exists that the congregations will follow their example and disregard weight management, a sort of permeated learning that is self-destructive.

20 Permeated Learning
Past to Present

Reflections

Discoveries in developing the permeated learning (Figure 18.1) model sustained with substantive living that is grounded in the data of the participants, helped to reflect and celebrate an ancestral heritage of health. Part of the reflections was upon the effects of desegregation upon the health of African-Americans. Then a retrospective application of the 3D pyramid brought to light unrealized secrets concerning ancestral knowledge to avoid type 2 diabetes mellitus (T2DM) and other diseases, especially valuable for one who is a pastor, scientist, and more applicable, have diabetes.

Legacy of Health (1888–1965)

The importance of ancestors in the participants understanding of T2DM provoked the recall of suppressed memories related to health. The suppression resulted from embarrassment from rearing in a home more primitive than of peers, and from experiences with desegregation. However, the study revealed the need for ancestors to model healthy living to the youth who will, in turn, become the ancestors emulated. Therefore, in reflection, is knowledge back to 1888 through Papa (Figures 14.1 and 20.1). That primitive upbringing reflected him; in that, we burned the wood that we cut on our property in similar ways to his upbringing. The water we drank until they ran dry came from wells that he dug. We ate the foods that he (we) raised, picked, fed, or hunted. Our access to more than 600 acres of forest, thickets, swamps, red dirt, and sandy white soil meant hard work, but healthy living and fun on Saturdays. Papa raised hogs, bees, and acres of black eye peas, purple hull peas, sweet potatoes, squash, okra, corn, cantaloupes, and "black diamond" red meat watermelons. We planted up to 40 acres annually with a mule or two, and an assortment of plows. However, in the mix came stories from 1888. Papa mentioned Indians seen from time to time in the backwoods, and some of them he called "Black Indians." This researcher never knew who they were but did not question it for two reasons. First, the fear of a swatting for asking the question, but even more, most of the things in the rural world was an enigma. For example, Papa was 70 years old when he

150 *The Theory: Permeated Learning Emergence*

fathered this researcher and had three other children afterward. He was short, bow-legged, with a black face, yellow torso, and brown legs. His uncle, Uncle Mitchell, a World War I veteran, and his daughter Cuten (cousin) Farris, looked like Indians. Both had beautiful yellow skin, nose shaped like an Indian, and black wavy hair. Papa showed the researcher the wagon trails that his daddy would take once a year for supplies in Nacogdoches Texas, approximately a 120-mile round-trip.

With a sixth-grade education, Papa was simple and lived in a dualistic world of his own. Things were either black or white, yes or no, on or off. For example, somehow (he did not say how) he was enlisted in the military for World War I; he told the researcher and his smaller sibling, while sitting around the wood-burning stove in the living room, of the many prejudices that he faced on his train trip from East Texas to New York. He said he got off the train and, "heard all of that commotion of hooting and hollering," reported Yvonne, the researcher's sister-in-law, who admired his longevity. He found out that the war was over and came back to his farm. In 1985 at the age of 97, following his death, with efforts to procure a flag for his services in the military, that same sister-in-law found that he never bothered with the discharge processes from the army. For him, there was no war, no service. So, what does this have to do with T2DM? The fact is he left a legacy from his generation of hard work that reduced obesity and diabetes. However, he also left a legacy of physical exercise (see Figure 20.1) despite having a labor-intensive

Figure 20.1 Ancestors Legacy of Health, "Hard Hustles," circa 1910. Photo: Curtesy of Earnest and Yvonne Redwine.

life, apparently inherited from his father. Knowledge from this study revealed the need for ancestors to pass along healthy means of managing T2DM to the youth. In an epiphany came the realization that Papa, with his sixth-grade education, had done more than the researcher did with his children.

Figure 20.1 is a group photo of Papa, and based on the words of an older brother, Wilmer (now deceased), was Grandpa Henry, along with, some, Negro League baseball team. Older siblings also mentioned that the Negro League that produced Jackie Robinson wanted Papa to join it, but he refused to leave his farm. Another event removed any doubt about his health. The researcher, at the age of 12 years, which means Papa was 82, was challenged when an older nephew (Henry, aka Butch), and the older brother, Wilmer, now deceased, encouraged Papa to race the researcher for about 40 to 50 yards. To this day, this nephew talks about Papa beating the researcher in that race. The researcher probably let him win, but the point is, "how many 82-year-olds can run respectably enough to look as though they can win?" Fittingly, Butch Henry plays intermural baseball in Denver, Colorado, and he has gone to many championship tournaments over the years. A cousin we called "Bimbo," though his name was Roger, loved baseball and seemed to take up where Papa left off. Bimbo was the son of Papa's uncle Columbus, the brother of Uncle Mitchell though neither looked like the other. Roger's nephew, Stanly Redwine, the son of C. C. Redwine, is the head track coach at Kansas University, former Olympic head coach, and in the Kansas Athletics Hall of Fame. However, desegregation caused many youths the age of the researcher to suppress knowledge of the culture of their ancestors, by causing feelings of shame for seemingly African-Americans' slave mentality of conducting business. In retrospect, the need existed to transition from the old to the new. That is, during the desegregation, African-Americans needed wise elders (male and female) to put things into perspective by explaining what was, and why, and what needed to be, going forward. Instead, desegregation unceremoniously disenfranchised African-Americans of their heritage, including topics related to healthy living.

The Second Diaspora, Health (1966 to Present)

There is a striking resemblance between the African diaspora and desegregation for many African-Americans, especially concerning health. Although desegregation was appropriate, the poor execution, if not purposely orchestrated, was shameful. Desegregation began during the researcher's first year of public school while in the first grade at the age of seven. By the age of nine, in the third grade, came the culture shock of the White school. There were only two years to observe African-Americans in a segregated school environment, with African-American administrators, teachers, bus drivers, and other entrepreneurs. Many things were bad and provided a good reason for integration, but African-Americans did not deserve the observed unfair treatment in the process of desegregation. There are good memories of Christmas plays, the introduction to "secular music," like Jimmy Mack as opposed to Gospel music at churches and country music on the radio—because there were no Black Gospel stations.

Finally, baseball was the highlighted sports activity; that began with after-school practices, on the baseball field at the rear of Goldsberry School. Reflection on the practices brings back memories of a baseball zooming from player to player, with lightning speed, and athletes with quick reflexes and dexterity, and frightening to a seven-year-old. The baseball field was simple, but functional, with the anticipations of something special about to happen. One day, it must have been a game day, Bimbo had on one of the school's beautiful black and gold baseball uniforms, instead of the drab white practice one. However, abruptly in 1963, officials gave African-American parents one of two choices. Starting the next school year, they could send all of their children to the White public school or spend half the first year and the others the next year. Our parents decided to do, as did most of the community, like Jacob in the Bible did with his family when facing the imminent threat from his brother Esau. Jacob sent the older children ahead of, the younger ones, seemingly, more loved. The big difference was that Esau had more mercy than the White schools of desegregation. All of the African-Americans sent to the White schools, the first year, had to repeat their previous grade, except the ones mixed with another race, as seen by their light skin. Consider the following previous statements:

> The social constructs of African-Americans began with slavery that initially imported only young virulent men, who were not fully indoctrinated in the African culture (Frazier, 1963). Furthermore, no more than five could congregate without a White man in the presence, which continued until introduced to the White man's religion (Frazier, 1963). These young men never fully gained the experiences of tribal customs, which made it easy to forget most of them.

The reality is desegregation unceremoniously dismissed an entire generation of African-Americans culture, especially detrimental to health. Although African-Americans maintained and still maintain that heritage of Afro-Theism through the African-American churches, most of the younger ones seem to have lost the will to pursue baseball like ancestors, which provided a means of preserving their health. Desegregation should have transitioned with a celebration of African-Americans doing an amazing job of educating its youth, physically and mentally, despite a lack of support from those with resources in the White community. Instead, authorities told African-Americans directly or indirectly that all of their school systems were worthless. As a result, most youths did not dare go to historically Black colleges and universities once they graduated from high school. In part, this study revitalizes the African-American heritage by revealing the importance of ancestry through the production of the 3D pyramid (Figure 18.1) model for evaluating an understanding of T2DM from their perspective. The development of this model grounded in the data of the participants awakens the need to revisit African-Americans' former instinctive means of combating T2DM and other health issues that the nature of desegregation caused the culture to suppress.

Pastor and Scientist Combination

The 3D pyramid model of permeated learning (Figure 18.1) shows that faith concerning diabetes mellitus is the primary link between the processes of T2DM. Being a pastor accentuates the importance of faith, as it helps individuals cope with T2DM. Additionally, as a scientist comes the realization of the implications of inefficient or ineffective insulin, high glucose, and hemoglobin A_{1c} values in relationship to T2DM. Finally, as an African-American with diabetes comes an appreciation of the 3D pyramid (Figure 18.1) that seamlessly helps the researcher as both a pastor and a scientist. This study uses faith like older pastors who related it to the belief concerning any assumptions. Pastors in the Pentecostal church are notorious for using faith in conjunction with sitting in a chair. They say, "you must have faith to believe that the chair will not collapse when taking a seat." Here, faith is the compartmentalization expressed by the participants who demonstrated their belief about their condition based on their ancestor's condition with T2DM. The 3D pyramid (Figure 18.1) gives a frame of reference to evaluate personal beliefs about T2DM, and even better, it provides a visual map to transforming or changing, terms currently used, but permeated learning best describes. As a scientist, it is irresistible to tests the model in the circumstances other than with diabetes. For example, when feeling stressed to an extreme, a mental image of the model appears, and the self-assessment ensues to determine the damage to the faith. Assessing other situations based on the 3D permeated learning pyramid (Figure 18.1) model is also common.

For example, at that time (2014), six-year-old Jayla (aka Punkin), one of two granddaughters, was traumatized by a doctor at the age of two. Base upon the 3D pyramid (Figure 18.1), with the fear (emotion) of doctors, there is one of the three directions of movement: either fix (positive action), fatalism (negative action), or faith (precautionary action). Based on the 3D pyramid (Figure 18.1), she will react by making a comparison to ancestors or family (see Figure 13.4), primarily her mother. Fixing the problem is not an option since she cannot erase the event; fatalism, which means avoiding the doctors, is just as bad. The best choice is to speak and model confidence when discussing or associating health issues with clinicians, which will "sensitize" her with knowledge and actions that build her faith or trust in the doctors. Without her knowing the reason, Punkin's mother, the youngest of three daughters, is encouraged by the researcher to model confidence through verbal communication with her daughter.

How to foster change personally? As a pastor, with the realization that the African-American community has suffered second cultural losses of identity through desegregation, it is imperative to establish camaraderie through age-categorized physical activities such as softball, which could be reintroduced to aid in managing or avoiding diabetes. Therefore, as an African-American pastor, this study is a reminder of the importance of celebrating a heritage that supports physical activity in managing diabetes while using the 3D pyramid (Figure 18.1) to monitor changes. The intent is to present the idea to the pastors who are working with the American Diabetes Association (ADA) as facilitators in support groups at local churches. As a scientist, the best opportunity to exhibit the use of the 3D pyramid (Figure 18.1) for African-Americans is through presentations, as discussed in Chapter 19. Currently, understanding as an adult educator, scientist, and pastor (neither required) is applied in conjunction with the 3D pyramid (Figure 18.1) to develop self-efficacy toward T2DM. Recalling that the self-efficacy branch is the "solutions" interaction joining "fix and faith," the researcher does exercises (old folks type) daily, takes glucose readings, and takes the prescribed medications. Finally, with the aid of the 3D model, inevitable failures result in reassessments and shorter-lived frustrations, knowing it is part of the process of permeated learning, whether it is complications leading to frustration, surrendering leading to fatalism, or any other interactions leading to one of the major categories. In either case, it is clear from the 3D pyramid (Figure 18.1), the "permeated learning" model, that "substantive living" is the motive and should be embellished with motivators toward self-efficacy in healthy living with T2DM.

21 Gaps Bridged
Permeated Learning Theory Applied

Bridging the Gaps in Literature

The literature review found gaps in four areas that need revisiting since the study is complete. Namely, the gaps in the literature were exclusive studies of African-Americans with type 2 diabetes mellitus (T2DM), and a theory of how their faith and knowledge evolved through social constructs, and the effects of spirituality. Except for spirituality, this study addressed all by focusing on the participants' social constructs. First, the study carved at the dearth of research explicitly related to African-Americans with T2DM, with a focus on one subculture. As for as the researcher knows, this is the first qualitative study completed using grounded theory exclusively with a subculture of African-American participants. Next, the study discovered that ancestors in the social constructs of a subculture had the greatest influence on what participants believed about their status with T2DM. Therefore, the biggest predictor of the actions, interactions, and emotions of the chosen African-American subculture is their faith or belief concerning their status with diabetes. Afro-Theism that resulted in the 3D pyramid (Figure 18.1) model represents the interaction between faith, knowledge, and social constructs. Finally, although faith resembles Cordova's (2011) spirituality, which is an important topic deserving an investigation for African-Americans, it was not the goal of this study.

This study lays the foundation for others to build upon it since only one subculture of African-Americans were considered, due to divisions along the lines of religious differences. However, divisions within the culture may not prove much different from the one in this study. This fact became more evident in a recent (2019) search to fellowship with a larger body of believers that resulted in a four-month pilgrimage to local churches that were separated ethnically, denominationally, socially, and mixtures of two or more. Amazingly, the greatest discovery was that African-Americans maintained a core of similarity with a nuance of differences based on the style of worship with usually one doctrinal difference that separated them into denominations.

Whereas others, primarily White-dominated churches, were separated more acutely with doctrinal differences. As a result, the selection of the Church of God in Christ (COGIC) denomination with more than five million members (Houdmann, 2012) in America that became the choice has even greater implications in the African-American culture. Since, at the time of the research, the choice resulted because of the potential impact of the number of church members and a familiarity with the denomination, and the recent pilgrimage seems not only to confirm but expands on that significance.

Nevertheless, despite addressing the dearth of literature in three of the four areas, the study is limited. The limitation is in the number of participants used to develop a theory of how Afro-Theistic faith, knowledge of T2DM, and Afro-Theistic social constructs worked together for this African-American subculture. This study followed the latest processes of the grounded theory methodology developed by Corbin and Strauss (2007), who considered theoretical saturation in developing a theory more important than the numbers of participants. As such, the study required thick and rich descriptions that saturated emerging categories from a few participants to answer the all-important question of "what is going on here?" Howbeit, the study leaves room for expansion upon the three gaps addressed in this study by using more participants, in the COGIC denomination, but also other subcultures in the African-American community. Also, spirituality in African-Americans with T2DM deserves a full study alone. Even so, the 3D pyramid (Figure 18.1) model in conjunction with the spirituality of African-Americans with T2DM segue in filling the gaps in the literature.

Theory Applied

The personal gain from the theory of permeated learning (PL), and the core category of substantive living as a motivator, is a case study of the theory's potential. Reflections on the daily battles with T2DM for the last five years has proven an accurate predictor of behavior and aid in managing the disease. Seeing personal trends of victories and failures leading to subsequent actions and interaction with faith or beliefs continually evolving serving as the captain, as predicted by PL, has led to a dependency on it for understanding and encouragement. Overall, understanding how permeated learning works has resulted in the slow loss of weight and T2DM management, despite setbacks. A national presentation of the theory at the 2016 American Society for Clinical Laboratory Scientist (ASCLS) presented the so-called, Old Folks exercises as a YouTube video, captured by the researcher's son at, https://www.youtube.com/watch?v=OcJtIRl62cY&t=709s, and the complete presentation he called "Dr. Gerald Redwine—ASCLS Presentation—812016." Through permeated learning, these have become a way to daily maintain control of health with the personal satisfaction of substantive living. These changes are far from perfect, and so far, resulted in an unrealized desire to lose 15 more pounds permanently.

However, permeated learning lends confidence that given time, it will come to pass while maintaining a personally defined substantive life. Until recently, one MAJOR hindrance was an addiction to sweets that the permeated learning theory allowed that admittance without feeling it was the end of the world. Taking a cue from, well, a televangelist, yes, that is correct, while scanning the channels, the researcher heard him mentioned a two-week fast from sugar, even sweeteners that serve as confusion to the body in knowing the intake of calories. Although he did not look the picture of health, accurate or not, it struck home as a process of permeated learning affecting the fix to "captain" faith tandem; in other words, self-efficacy, so why not give it a go? Knowing that fasting is part of the participants' church's culture and the researcher's background, and having statements about problems for those with diabetes come thoughts that this challenge could provide a positive and useful result with success. With or without success, permeated learning would occur.

Thankfully, after almost six decades the cravings and tolerance for extreme quantities of sweets were broken, even of nearly 20 years of the beloved sweeteners, one exclusively for more than a decade in coffee and oatmeal. What has happened? Apparently, during the two-week fast, the idea that this addiction was unbreakable without the loss of "substantive living" was deconstructed and redefined, somewhat. The thought of how good these tasted were there, but the joy of breaking the habit and fear of becoming addicted once more overpowered the return to that level of substantive living. This fear was a reality check of believing that when one has the cognition and the ability, yet continues that habit until death, that individual is an addict.

Perhaps this is an excellent time to mention the difference in permeation and Jack Mesirow's transformation. Most notably, the researcher believes that "permeated learning" must occur before "transformation." Further, it seems that "transformative learning" points toward lasting results while "permeated learning" speaks to the processes of learning in real-time. Stated differently, permeated knowledge speaks to change without expecting termination or perfection, only possibilities of achievement until *death*. For example, at this point is the realization that a return to old habits is not only possible but the easiest option; at the same time is the comprehended potential to redefine reality. Therefore, at present, the "permeated learning" theory has provided a sense of empowerment by providing a model of the processes or driving forces behind the decisions of those with diabetes and the knowledge that "substantive living" is the motivator. All without the risk of failure because that is part of the process of "permeated learning."

Consequently, empowerment means choices, which makes living adjustable to any life event with modification possible to the idea of self-defined "substantive living" through "permeated learning." Do coffee and oatmeal taste as sweet as it once did? Unequivocally no, on the other hand, putting the same amount of sweetener makes them seem too sugary. What has happened? Faith or belief has changed through processes of "permeated learning," and now is the opportunity to allow the adjustment to a new norm or standard defined as "substantive living."

The researcher wrote the last statement before August 2018. Around that time upon the promise weight loss from a bulletin at the primary care physician (PCP) office, the doctor granted permission and a warning that exercise MUST accompany the weight loss injections. Hoping this was the discovery of the "quick fix" Livia had thought existed, the researcher, as usual, went all-in until February 2019. What were the results? The researcher experienced weight loss at first, with over three miles of jogging per day until November 2018 when he noticed that his weight balanced to what it was before the weight loss injections. What happened? According to his "young" PCP during his next visit in January 2019, that was normal and expected because of muscle gain, and he was to keep it up. Then came a reality check from the researcher. First, being more than 60 years old, how much longer, could the jogging continue, and what would happen if he stopped. Second, the management of diabetes had not improved, and the same quantity of medicine was required. Finally, the researcher noticed that it did not matter what he did, his young doctor in the five to ten minutes of a rushed visit would either blame him for any failures or take credit for any successes.

As a result, in February 2019, the researcher decided to revert to what has worked in the past, which was the daily exercises mentioned earlier, and had continued through this failed trial and error, but noticed an increased craving for sweets, followed by a small gain in weight. Frustration! Fortunately, more recently (yesterday, April 23, 2019), following the news of the tremendous weight loss of a nephew-in-law, who has diabetes, is the permeation of doing as he did by eliminating sweets, bread, rice, and, potatoes from his diet. With adjustments to the existence of "substantive living," permeated learning is possible, which, of course, means that "faith" concerning living with T2DM will change. The battle continues. Here is an up to the minute before publication update. As of June 3, 2019, the researcher, even on such a regimented diet, found a way to gain weight. He found another addiction—walnuts; embarrassingly, three (3) pounds in one (1) week. What happened? Gained the weight back once more; however, the elevated glucose did NOT return, AND that is with one-half the medication. Permeated learning says that it is okay, and self-efficacy is yet in effect, with a simple modification in substantive living, by giving up the walnuts. What happened? As of yesterday, the weight loss of three (3) pounds, and the glucose with half the prescription is good. Permeated learning continues.

Permeated Learning Theory Applied 159

As a final application, the researcher's best results have come using permeated learning that emphasizes the importance of doing what others do in the culture who have modeled self-efficacy, which continues a trajectory *beyond* transformational learning. The resulting permeated learning theory provides a unique Afro-Theistic theory grounded in the data of members with diabetes from the COGIC subculture of African-Americans. It led to an understanding of how they construct knowledge about diabetes and provides means of dialogue with those outside the culture. It also provided reasonable responses to all questions, with graphic depictions of the all-important route to "self-efficacy," and an understanding of the "martyr's response."

A final observation. The researcher adherence to a "logocentric" ontology, a "constructivist" epistemology and a "theistic" paradigm, made bias a concern. Nevertheless, efforts to conduct an objective investigation of the participants ultimately revealed their "substantive living" ontology, a "permeated learning" epistemology, and "faith" as a paradigm relative to knowledge, and social constructs concerning T2DM that is different yet like the researcher's philosophy. With similar backgrounds, one would expect similarities, but the differences are indicators of objectiveness.

"Permeation before Transformation!"

References

ACS, ADA, AHS, & ASA. (2011). *Protecting patients: The personal responsibility coverage requirement.* The American Cancer Society, the American diabetes Association, the American Heart Association, & the American stroke Association. Retrieved from www.diabetes.org/assets/pdfs/advocacy/php-report.pdf.

ADA. (2011). *Diabetes: A national epidemic with deadly and costly complications.* Retrieved from Alexandria, VA: http://www.diabetes.org/assets/pdfs/advocacy/federal-legislative.pdf

ADA. (2013). *In my community: Project POWER.* Retrieved from http://www.diabetes.org/in-my-community/programs/african-american-programs/project-power.html

Asante, M. K. (1988). *Afrocentricity: The theory of social change.* Trenton, NJ: Africa World Press.

Baker, E. A., Kelly, C., Barnidge, E., Strayhorn, J., Schootman, M., Struthers, J., & Griffith, D. (2006). The garden of Eden: Acknowledging the impact of race and class in efforts to decrease obesity rates. *American Journal of Public Health, 96*(7), 1170–1174.

Bandura, A. (1966). Observational learning as a function of symbolization and incentive set. *Child Development, 37,* 499–506.

Bandura, A. (1971). *Social learning theory.* Morristown, NJ: General Learning Press.

Bandura, A. (1977). Self-efficacy: Toward a unifying theory of behavioral change. *Psychological Review, 84*(2), 191–215.

Bandura, A. (1989). Human agency in social cognitive theory. *American Psychologist, 44*(9), 1175–1184.

Baumgartner, L. M. (2000). *The incorporation of HIV/AIDS into identity over time* (9986900 Ed.D.), University of Georgia, Ann Arbor, MI. Retrieved from http://libproxy.txstate.edu/login?url=http://search.proquest.com/docview/304591932?accountid=5683; http://linksource.ebsco.com/linking.aspx?sid=ProQuest+Dissertations+%26+Theses+Full+Text&fmt=dissertation&genre=dissertations+%26+theses&issn=&volume=&issue=&date=2000-01-01&spage=&title=The+incorporation+of+HIV%2FAIDS+into+identity+over+time&atitle=&au=Baumgartner%2C+Lisa+Marie&isbn=9780599934153&jtitle=&btitle= ProQuest Dissertations & Theses Full Text database.

Baumgartner, L. M. (2011). The role of adult learning in coping with chronic illness. *New Directions for Adult and Continuing Education, 2011*(130), 7–16. doi:10.1002/ace.406

References

Bennett, E. E., & Bell, A. A. (2010). Paradox and promise in the knowledge society. In C. E. Kasworm, A. D. Rose, & J. M. Ross-Gordon (Eds.), *Handbook of adult and continuing education* (Vol. 2010 Edition). Thousand Oaks, CA: Sage Publications, Inc.

Birks, M., & Mills, J. (2011). *Grounded theory: A practical guide.* Thousand Oaks, CA: Sage Publications.

Blumer, H. (1969). *Symbolic interactionism: Perspective and method.* Englewood Cliffs, NJ: Prentice-Hall, Inc.

Bogdan, R., & Biklen, S. K. (2007). *Qualitative research for education: An introduction to theory and methods/Robert C. Bogdan, Sari Knopp Biklen* (5th ed.). Boston, MA: Pearson/Allyn and Bacon.

Boucouvalas, M., & Lawrence, R. L. (2010). Adult learning. In C. E. Kasworm, A. D. Rose, & J. M. Ross-Gordon (Eds.), *Handbook of adult and continuing education* (Vol. 2010 Edition, pp. 35–46). Thousand Oaks, CA: Sage Publications, Inc.

Bricker, P. L., Baron, R. J., Scheirer, J. J., DeWalt, D. A., Derrickson, J., Yunghans, S., & Gabbay, R. A. (2010). Collaboration in Pennsylvania: Rapidly spreading improved chronic care for patients to practices. *Journal of Continuing Education in the Health Professions, 30*(2), 114–125.

Brown, C. (1995). A world come of age. In T. Dowley (Ed.), *Introduction to the history of Christianity* (pp. 548–556). Singapore: First Fortress Press.

Bullon, S., Carey, S., Creese, S., Francis, G., Hargraves, O., Kirkland, F., . . . Sule, K. (2007). Macmillan English dictionary. In M. Rundell (Ed.), *Macmillan English Dictionary* (2nd ed.). https://www.macmillandictionary.com/dictionary/british/permeate

Bureau, U. S. C. (2002a). Table 1. United States—Race and Hispanic origin: 1790 to 1990. U.S. Department of Commerce Economics and Statistics Administration U.S. Census Bureau.

Bureau, U. S. C. (2002b). Table 4. South Region—Race and Hispanic origin: 1790 to 1990. U.S. Department of Commerce Economics and Statistics Administration U.S. Census Bureau.

CDC. (2011). *National diabetes fact sheet: National estimates and general information on diabetes and prediabetes.* Retrieved from Atlanta, GA: www.diabetes.org/diabetes-basics/prevention/pre-diabetes/how-to-prevent-pre-diabetes.html

CDC. (2012a). *Diabetes report card.* Retrieved from Atlanta, GA: http://www.cdc.gov/diabetes/pubs/pdf/DiabetesReportCard.pdf

CDC. (2012b, October 5, 2012). *National diabetes prevention program.* Retrieved from http://www.cdc.gov/diabetes/prevention/about.htm

Charmaz, K. (2011). Grounded theory methods in social justice research. In *Five ways of doing qualitative analysis* (p. 21). New York, London: The Guilford Press.

Corbin, J. M., & Strauss, A. L. (2007). *Basics of qualitative research: Techniques and procedures for developing grounded theory* (Kindle Edition). Thousand Oaks, CA: Sage Publications.

Cordova, C. M. (2011). *The lived experience of spirituality among Type 2 diabetic mellitus patients with macrovascular and/or microvascular complications* (3454704 Ph.D.), The Catholic University of America, Ann Arbor. Retrieved from http://libproxy.txstate.edu/login?url=http://search.proquest.com/

References

docview/871100620?accountid=5683; http://linksource.ebsco.com/linking. aspx?sid=ProQuest+Dissertations+%26+Theses+Full+Text&fmt=dissertation &genre=dissertations+%26+theses&issn=&volume=&issue=&date=2011- 01-01&spage=&title=The+Lived+Experience+of+Spirituality+among+ Type+2+Diabetic+Mellitus+Patients+with+Macrovascular+and%2For+Mi crovascular+Complications&atitle=&au=Cordova%2C+Cynthia+M.& isbn=9781124646121&jtitle=&btitle= ProQuest Dissertations & Theses Full Text database.

Cornwall, A., & Jewkes, R. (1995). What is participatory research? *Social Science & Medicine, 41*(12), 1667–1676.

Creswell, J. W. (2007). *Qualitative inquiry & research design: Choosing among five approaches/John W. Creswell* (2nd ed.). Thousand Oaks, CA: Sage Publications.

Crotty, M. (1998). *The foundations of social research.* London, Thousand Oaks, CA, New Delhi: Sage Publications.

Davidson, J., & Davidson, F. (2003). *Bandura's social cognitive theory: An introduction.* San Luis Obispo, CA: Davidson Films, Inc. [Streaming Video]. Retrieved from video.alexanderstreet.com/watch/bandura-s-social-cognitive-theory-an-introduction database

Davis, E. M., Clark, J. M., Carrese, J. A., Gary, T. L., & Cooper, L. A. (2005). Racial and socioeconomic differences in the weight-loss experiences of obese women. *American Journal of Public Health, 95*(9), 1539–1543.

Davis-Smith, M. (2007). Implementing a diabetes prevention program in a rural African-American church. *Journal of the National Medical Association, 99*(4), 440–446.

DeNavas-Walt, C., Proctor, B. D., & Smith, J. C. (2011). *Income, poverty, and health insurance coverage in the United States: 2011.* Retrieved from Washington, DC: http://www.census.gov/prod/2012pubs/p60-243.pdf

Derrida, J. (1976). *Of grammatology* (G. C. Spivak, Trans.). Baltimore, MD and London: The Johns Hopkins University Press.

Dewey, J. (1982). My pedagogic creed. *Language Arts, 59*, 539–544.

Eltis, D. (2008). The U.S. transatlantic slave trade, 1644–1867: An assessment. *Civil war history, 53*(4), 347–378. doi:10.1353/cwh.0.0033

Ennis, S. R., Ríos-Vargas, M., & Albert, N. G. (2011). *The Hispanic population: 2010 census briefs.* Retrieved from Washington, DC: http://www.census.gov/prod/cen2010/briefs/c2010br-04.pdf

Enns, P. (1989). *The Moody handbook of theology.* Chicago, IL: Moody Press.

Estate of Dr. Martin Luther King Jr. (n.d.). I've been to the mountaintop. *American rhetoric: top 100 speeches.* Retrieved from http://www.americanrhetoric.com/speeches/mlkivebeentothemountaintop.htm

Exegetical Dictionary of the New Testament, V 1: Aarōn-Henōch. (1990). Grand Rapids: Eerdmans.

Fraenkel, J. R., Wallen, N. E., & Hyun, H. H. (2012). *How to design and evaluate research in education* (8th ed.). New York: The McGraw-Hill Companies, Inc.

Frazier, E. F. (1963). *The Negro church in America.* New York: Schocken Books.

Freire, P. (1998). *Pedagogy of freedom: Ethics, democracy, and civic courage/ Paulo Freire; translated by Patrick Clarke; foreword by Donaldo Macedo;*

introduction by Stanley Aronowitz. Lanham, MD: Rowman & Littlefield Publishers, Inc.

Gaillard, T. (2007). Faith-based adult learning initiatives for diabetes education in the African American community. *Adult Learning, 18*(1/2), 6–8.

Gasque, W. W. (1995). The church expands: Jerusalem to Rome. In T. Dowley (Ed.), *Introduction to the history of Christianity* (pp. 57–81). Singapore: First Fortress Press.

Gay, L. R., Mills, G. E., & Airasian, P. W. (2006). *Educational research: Competence for analysis and applications*. Upper Saddle River, NJ: Pearson, Merrill Prentice Hall.

Giles, M. S. (2010). Howard Thurman, black spirituality, and critical race theory in higher education. *Journal of Negro Education, 79*(3), 354–365.

Glaser, B. G., & Strauss, A. L. (1967). *The discovery of grounded theory; strategies for qualitative research [by] Barney G. Glaser and Anselm L. Strauss [Kindle PC version]*. Retrieved from Amazon.com

Glesne, C. (2011). *Becoming qualitative researchers: An introduction* (4th ed.). Boston, MA: Pearson education.

Greene, M. (1995). *Releasing the imagination (Part 1: Creating possibilities)*. San Francisco, CA: Jossey-Bass.

Grissom-II, A. C. (2013, 3/27/2013). Church of God in Christ (COGIC). *The encyclopedia of Arkansas history & culture*. Retrieved from http://www.encyclopediaofarkansas.net/encyclopedia/entry-detail.aspx?entryID=2296

Hansman, C. A., & Mott, V. W. (2010). Adult learners. In C. E. Kasworm, A. D. Rose, & J. M. Ross-Gordon (Eds.), *Handbook of: Adult and continuing education* (Vol. 2010 Edition). Thousand Oaks, CA: Sage Publications, Inc.

Hayes, D. L. (2012). *Forms in the fiery furnace: African-American spirituality*. Maryknoll, NY: Orbis Books.

Hixson, L., Hepler, B. B., & Kim, M. O. (2011). *The White Population: 2010 census briefs*. Retrieved from Washington, DC: http://www.census.gov/prod/cen2010/briefs/c2010br-05.pdf

The Holy Bible: English Standard Version, Containing the Old and New Testaments (ESV). (2011). (ESV text edition). Wheaton, IL: Crossway.

Horton, M., & Jacobs, D. (Eds.). (2003). *The Myles Horton reader: Education for social change*. Knoxville, TN: University of Tennessee Press.

Houdmann, S. M. (2012). *Is the Church of God in Christ (COGIC) a good, biblical church?* Retrieved from http://www.gotquestions.org/COGIC.html

Hurston, Z. N. (1981). *The sanctified Church: The four who were writings of Zora Neale Hurston*. Berkeley, CA: Turtle Island Foundation.

Kasworm, C. E., Rose, A. D., & Ross-Gordon, J. M. (Eds.). (2010). *Handbook of adult and continuing education* (Vol. 2010 Edition). Thousand Oaks, CA: Sage Publications, Inc.

Kessler, D., Dubouloz, C.-J., Urbanowski, R., & Egan, M. (2009). Meaning perspective transformation following stroke: The process of change. *Disability & Rehabilitation, 31*(13), 1056–1065.

Kiawi, E., Edwards, R., Shu, J., Unwin, N., Kamadjeu, R., & Claude Mbanya, J. (2006). Knowledge, attitudes, and behavior relating to diabetes and its main risk factors among urban residents in Cameroon: A qualitative survey. *Ethnicity & Disease, 16*(Spring 2006), 503–509.

Kincheloe, J. L., & McLaren, P. (2008). Rethinking critical theory and qualitative research. In N. K. Denzin & Y. S. Lincoln (Eds.), *The landscape of qualitative research* (Vol. 3). Thousand Oaks, CA: Sage Publications, Inc.

Knowles, M. S. (1970). *The modern practice of adult education; andragogy versus pedagogy, by Malcolm S. Knowles.* New York: Association Press.

Knowles, M. S., Holton, E. F., III, & Swanson, R. A. (2011). *The adult learner [electronic resource]: The definitive classic in adult education and human resource development.* Retrieved from http://catalog.library.txstate.edu.libproxy.txstate.edu/record=b2160985~S1a

Kübler-Ross, E. (1970). *On death and dying.* New York: Collier Books/Macmillan Publishing Co.

Kuhn, D. (1999). A developmental model of critical thinking. *Educational Researcher, 28*(2), 16–26.

Lugo, L., Stencel, S., Green, J., Smith, G., Pond, D. C. a. A., Miller, T., . . . Ralston, M. (2008). *U.S. Religious landscape survey religious beliefs and practices: Diverse and politically relevant* (pp. 469–493). Retrieved from http://libproxy.txstate.edu/login?url=http://search.ebscohost.com/login.aspx?direct=true&db=edsoai&AN=edsoai.712284466&site=eds-live&scope=site; http://religions.pewforum.org/pdf/report2-religious-landscape-study-full.pdf; http://health-equity.pitt.edu/1020/; http://worldcat.org/search?q=on:PIT+http://health-equity.pitt.edu/cgi/oai2+DCG_ENTIRE_REPOSITORY+CNTCOLL

Maine State Dept. of Human Services, A. B. o. H. (1997). *Report on results of focus groups conducted with people with disabilities.* Retrieved from http://libproxy.txstate.edu/login?url=http://search.ebscohost.com/login.aspx?direct=true&db=eric&AN=ED420123&site=eds-live&scope=site

Mead, G. H., & Morris, C. W. (1934). *Mind, self & society from the standpoint of a social behaviorist [by] George H. Mead.* Edited, with introduction, by Charles W. Morris. Chicago, IL: The University of Chicago Press.

Melancon, J., Oomen-Early, J., & del Rincon, L. M. (2009). Using the PEN-3 model to assess knowledge, attitudes, and beliefs about diabetes Type 2 among Mexican American and Mexican Native men and women in North Texas. *International Electronic Journal of Health Education, 12,* 203–221.

Merriam, S. B. (2009). *Qualitative research: A guide to design and implementation.* San Francisco, CA: Jossey-Bass.

Mezirow, J. (1991). *Transformative dimensions of adult learning/Jack Mezirow* (1st ed.). San Francisco, CA: Jossey-Bass.

Mezirow, J. (1997). Transformative learning: Theory to practice. *New Directions for Adult & Continuing Education, 74*(5), 5–12.

Mills, G. E. (2007). *Action research: A guide for the teacher researcher* (3rd ed.). Upper Saddle River, NJ: Pearson, Merrill Prentice Hall.

NDEP. (2011). *The diabetes epidemic among African-Americans.* Retrieved from Bethesda, MD: http://www.ndep.nih.gov/media/fs_africanam.pdf

Norris, T., Vines, P. L., & Hoeffel, E. M. (2012). *The American Indian and Alaska Native Population: 2010 census briefs.* Retrieved from Washington, DC: http://www.census.gov/prod/cen2010/briefs/c2010br-10.pdf

Ntiri, D. W., & Stewart, M. (2009). Transformative learning intervention: Effect on functional health literacy and diabetes knowledge in older African Americans. *Gerontology & Geriatrics Education, 30*(2), 100–113.

References

Omi, M., & Winant, H. (2006). Chapter 22: Racial Formation in the United States: From the 1960s to the 1990s. In D. Grusky & S. Szelenyi (Eds.), *Inequality Reader: Contemporary & Foundational Readings in Race, Class, & Gender* (pp. 197–202). Taylor & Francis Ltd..

Paris, P. J. (1995). *The spirituality of African peoples*. Minneapolis, MN: Fortress Press.

Patton, M. Q. (2002). *Qualitative research and evaluation methods* (3rd ed.). Thousand Oaks, CA: Sage.

Prasad, J. (2007). *Derrida: The father of deconstruction*. Retrieved from http://newderrida.wordpress.com/2007/11/19/some-key-terms/

Ramm, B. (1970). *Protestant biblical interpretation: A textbook of hermeneutics*. Grand Rapids, MI: Baker Book House.

Range, C. F., Jr., Young, C., Ross, G. R., & Winbush, R. L. H. (Eds.). (1973). *Official manual with the doctrines and discipline of the Church Of God In Christ; 1973* (1992 ed.). Memphis, TN: Church of God in Christ.

Rastogi, S., Johnson, T. D., Hoeffel, E. M., & Drewery, M. P., Jr. (2011). *The Black population: 2010 census briefs*. Retrieved from Washington, DC: http://www.census.gov/prod/cen2010/briefs/c2010br-06.pdf

Redwine, G. D. (2015). *Type 2 diabetes mellitus (DM) in an African-American subculture: Grounded theory of Afro-Theistic faith, knowledge, and Afro-Theistic social constructs*. San Marcos, TX: Texas State University. https://digital.library.txstate.edu/handle/10877/5538

Roger, V. L., Go, A. S., Lloyd-Jones, D. M., Adams, R. J., Berry, J. D., Brown, T. M., . . . Wylie-Rosett, J. (2010). Heart disease and stroke statistics 2011 update: A report from the American Heart Association. *Circulation, 123*. Retrieved from Heart Disease and Stroke Statistics—2011 Update1 website: doi:10.1161/CIR.0b013e3182009701

Rohde, R. E. (2010). *Methicillin resistant Staphylococcus aureus (MRSA): Knowledge, learning and adaptation* (Ph.D.), Texas State University, San Marcos, TX. Retrieved from http://libproxy.txstate.edu/login?url=http://proquest.umi.com/pqdweb?did=2172194911&Fmt=7&clientId=11421&RQT=309&VName=PQD

Ruder, K., Blank, M., Hale, B., Nienow, D., & Rollins, K. (2007). *The collective leadership framework: A workbook for cultivated and sustaining community change*. Battle Creek, MI: W. K. Kellogg Foundation.

Ryrie, C. C. (1995). *Basic theology: A popular systematic guide to understanding biblical truth*. USA, Canada, England: Victor Books.

Samad, A. A. (2013). *Centennial: Celebrating 100 years of Phi Beta Sigma Fraternity, Inc*. Washington, DC: Beta Sigma Fraternity, Inc.

Saydah, S. H., Fradkin, J., & Cowie, C. C. (2004). Poor control of risk factors for vascular disease among adults with previously diagnosed diabetes. *JAMA: Journal of the American Medical Association, 291*(3), 335–342. doi:10.1001/jama.291.3.335

Smith, A. B. (1893). *An Autobiography: The Story of the Lord's Dealings with Mrs. Amanda Smith, the Colored Evangelist*. Chicago, IL: Meyer & Brother.

Smith, M. K. (2002). Malcolm Knowles, informal adult education, self-direction and andragogy. In *The encyclopedia of informal education* (Vol. 2011). www.infed.org/thinkers/et-knowl.htm

Summers, R. (1995). *Essentials of New Testament Greek*. Nashville, TN: Broadman & Holman.

Taylor, L. M. (2010). *An examination of potential influences on the success of prediabetes service provision* (Ph.D., University of Alberta, Canada. Retrieved from NR62924 http://libproxy.txstate.edu/login?url=http://search.proquest.com/docview/762753002?accountid=5683 ProQuest Dissertations & Theses (PQDT)

Turner, R. (1995). The color complex: Intraracial discrimination in the workplace. *Labor Law Journal, 46*(11), 678–684.

Two Feathers, J. G. (2005). *The development, implementation and results of the reach Detroit diabetes lifestyle intervention for African Americans and Latinos* (Doctor of Philosophy), University of Michigan, Detroit. Retrieved from http://search.proquest.com/docview/305423399?accountid=5683 ProQuest Dissertations and Theses database. (305423399)

U.S. Census Bureau. (2012). Statistical abstract of the United States: 2012 (Tables 76 and 77). Washington, DC: U.S. Government Printing Office.

Valencia, R. R. (1997). *The Evolution of deficit thinking: Educational thought and practice*. London, Washington, DC: The Falmer Press.

Vella, J. (2002). *Learning to listen learning to teach: The power of dialogue in educating adults*. San Francisco, CA: Josie-Bass.

Wade, S. D. (2005). *Evaluation of an African American faith-based diabetes education program*. (D.N.Sc.), University of Tennessee Health Science Center, Retrieved from http://libproxy.txstate.edu/login?url=http://search.ebscohost.com/login.aspx?direct=true&db=ccm&AN=2009711365&site=eds-live&scope=site Available from EBSCOhost ccm database.

Waldron, C. (2008). Bishop Charles E. Blake Elected COGIC's Presiding Bishop. *Jet, 114*(22), 24. Retrieved from http://search.ebscohost.com.libproxy.txstate.edu/login.aspx?direct=true&db=f6h&AN=35657438&site=eds-live&scope=site

Washington, J. R., Jr. (1964). *Black religion: The Negro and Christianity in the United States*. Boston, MA: Beacon Press.

Watson, J. (2002). *Martyrs of Columbine: Faith and the politics of tragedy*. Gordonsville, VA: Palgrave Macmillan.

Weaver, E. H. (2003). The metamorphosis of C. H. Mason: Origins of black Pentecostal churches in Tennessee. *West Tennessee Historical Society Papers, 57*, 35–57.

Weiler, D. M. (2007). *The socio-cultural influences and process of living with diabetes for the migrant Latino adult*. (3283945 Ph.D.), The University of Arizona, Ann Arbor, MI. Retrieved from http://libproxy.txstate.edu/login?url=http://search.proquest.com/docview/304895320?accountid=5683; http://linksource.ebsco.com/linking.aspx?sid=ProQuest+Dissertations+%26+Theses+Full+Text&fmt=dissertation&genre=dissertations+%26+theses&issn=&volume=&issue=&date=2007-01-01&spage=&title=The+socio-cultural+influences+and+process+of+living+with+diabetes+for+the+migrant+Latino+adult&atitle=&au=Weiler%2C+Dawn+Marie&isbn=9780549274377&jtitle=&btitle= ProQuest Dissertations & Theses Full Text database.

Whitehead, J. (2001a). COGIC history series: Bishop Charles Harrison Mason. In J. Whitehead (Ed.), *Church of God in Christ: The official quarterly guide: Senior YPWW* (Vol. 37). Memphis, TN: Church of God in Christ Publishing House.

Whitehead, J. (2001b). COGIC history series: History of education. In J. Whitehead (Ed.), *Church of God in Christ: The official quarterly guide: Senior YPWW* (Vol. 37). Memphis, TN: Church of God in Christ Publishing House.

Williams, A., Manias, E., Liew, D., Gock, H., & Gorelik, A. (2012). Working with CALD groups: Testing the feasibility of an intervention to improve medication self- management in people with kidney disease, diabetes, and cardiovascular disease. *Renal Society of Australasia Journal, 8*(2), 62–69.

Wood, A. S. (1995). The methodists. In T. Dowley (Ed.), *Introduction to the history of Christianity* (p. 453). Minneapolis, MN: First Fortress Press.

Wood, D., Pilisuk, M., & Uren, E. (1973). The Martyr's personality: An experimental investigation. *Journal of Personality and Social Psychology, 25*(2), 177–186. doi:10.1037/h0033969

Wright, D. F. (1995). The montanists. In T. Dowley (Ed.), *Introduction to the history of Christianity* (p. 87). Singapore: First Fortress Press.

Zuck, R. B. (1991). *Basic Bible interpretation*. Wheaton, IL: Victor Bks.

Index

Note: **Bold** page numbers refer to tables and *italic* page numbers refer to figures.

acidosis 72
ADA *see* American Diabetes Association (ADA)
adult education theory 36
African-American community 12, 17, 154
African-American subcultures 25–6, 35, 53, 57, 156
African diaspora and desegregation 151–3
Afro-Theism 4, 16–18, 54–5, 155; beliefs 38; constructivism 20–3; faith *18*, 18–20, 38, 140; social constructs 140, 141; subcultures 38; substantive living (*see* substantive living)
Afro-Theistic symbolic interactionism 76–7, *77*; distractions 78; promoting healthy life 77
American Diabetes Association (ADA) 35, 40, 146, 148, 154
American Society for Clinical Laboratory Science (ASCLS) 51, 156
ancestors, mentors 91–2
anxiety 11, 45
Arminius, Jacobus 16, 17, 54
Asante, M. K. 19, 54–5, 136

Baker, E. A. 37, 38
Bandura, A. 53, 138
Baptist Church denomination 27, 29, 35
Baumgartner, L. M. 45, 138
Biklen, S. K. 43
Birks, M. 46
Black church 17, 54
Black spirituality 19

Blank, M. 38
Blumer, H. 53, 57
Bogdan, R. 43
Boucouvalas, M. 35
Bricker, P. L. 51

Calvin, John 16, 17
Centers for Disease Control and Prevention 40
Charmaz, K. 46
Christianity 50, 54, 62, 70, 95
chronic sufferer 45
Church of God in Christ (COGIC) 2, 7–9; denomination 28–9 (*see also* member, COGIC denomination); double marginalization 34–5; "father" 14; history and researcher 26–31; interviews 10–11; participants 11; purpose 39–40; rapport with participants 12–14; research questions 40–2; subculture 12–14; support 34
close-knit community 11
code statistics **108–9**
coding *81*, 81–2
comparative analysis 46–7, 96
conscientization (Freire) 38
constructivism, Afro-Theism 20–3; *see also* social constructivism
Corbin, J. M. 44, 46, 47, 79, 81, 84, 156
Cordova, C. M. 10, 43, 143, 155
coronary heart disease (CHD) 40, 51
credibility 83–4
Creswell, J. W. 46
critical race theory (CRT) 19
Crotty, M. 44, 56
cultural exclusiveness 37, 42

Index

Darwin, C. 26
data analysis 79–80, 84; coding 81, 81–2; credibility and trustworthiness 83–4; diagrams 82–3, 83; field notes 80, 80; memo writing 82
data collection 9, 10
data triangulation 84
Davis, E. M. 26
Davis-Smith, M. 26, 41, 51
decision-making process 26, 67, 76, 91, 93, 94, 104, 138
del Rincon, L. M. 41
Derrida, J. 56
Dewey, J. 3, 25, 45
diabetes 7–8, 43, 51; and coronary heart disease 40; educator 51–2; prediabetes and 51; support 34; workshop 13; *see also* type 2 diabetes mellitus (T2DM)
diabetes education 139–40; Afro-Theistic faith and 140
diagrams 82–3, 83
distractions, health 78
divine healing 35
doctors, mentors 99–101
double marginalization 34–5

Eltis, D. 18, 136
ethnicity, National Diabetes Statistics 36, 36–7

faith 97–8, 107–12, **108**, 136–7; Afro-Theism 18, 18–20; fatalism 114–15; fear 113–14, 122; fix 112–13, 116–18; frustration 115–16, 125–6; substantive living 107–16, 131–2
family, mentors 92–4
fatalism 96–7, 126–8; faith 114–15; fear 120–1; frustration 123–5; substantive living 126–8, 133
fear 86, 119; affectivity 89–91, 90; catalyst 87, 87–8; factors 88, 89; faith 113–14, 122; fatalism 120–1; fix 119–20; substantive living 119–22, 132
field notes 80, 80
fix 96, 116; faith 112–13, 116–18; fear 119–20; frustration 118–19; substantive living 116–19, 132
Freire, P. 38
frustration 102–3, 123; faith 115–16, 125–6; fatalism 123–5; fix 118–19; substantive living 123–6, 133

Gaillard, T. 26, 41–2
Gasque, W. W. 54
Giles, M. S. 28, 136
Glaser, B. G. 44, 45
Godin Leisure-Time Exercise Questionnaire (GLTEQ) 45
"Grannie Reen" 7, 143
Greene, M. 28
Gregory (Pope) 17
grounded theory 44–7

Hale, B. 38
Hayes, D. L. 55
healthy life, promoting 77
holiness 29, 31, 35
Holton, E. F., III 19
Horton, M. 25, 38
Hurston, Z. N. 19, 136

Inspiration 9 80, 83, 84
internalized racism and color- caste hierarchy 54
interview preparation 10–11

Jacobs, D. 25, 38
Jones, C. P. 29

Kessler, D. 44
knowledge 137–8; faith 112–16; fatalism 128; fear 120–2; fix 117–19; frustration 124–6
Knowles, M. S. 9, 19, 20, 56, 84, 142
Kübler-Ross, E. 143
Kuhn, D. 40

Lawrence, R. L. 35
Legacy of Health (1888–1965) 149–51, 150

Mapping research activities; Extracting meaning from the data; Maintaining momentum; and Opening communication (MEMO) 46
"martyr response" 40
Mason, C. H. 50
MAXQDA 79–82, 84
Mead, G. H. 45, 53, 57
medical laboratory scientist (MLS) 51, 55
medical technology (MT) 51
member, COGIC denomination: Arianna 60–2; Carlos 68–71; Glenn 62–5; Livia 65–8; Nick 71–5
memo writing 82

Memphis Commercial Appeal 30
mentors 91, *91*, 137; ancestors 91–2; doctors and pastors 98–102; family 92–4; social figures 94–5
Merriam, S. B. 43
Mexican-Americans 1, 25, 41
Mezirow, J. 41, 52, 138, 144
Mills, J. 46
Montanists 54
Morris, C. W. 45, 53

National Diabetes Statistics **36**, 36–7
neuropathy 7
Nienow, D. 38
Ntiri, D. W. 41

Omi, M. 19
Oomen-Early, J. 41
The Origin of Species (Charles) 26

paradigm 55–6
Paris, P. J. 55
participants 9, 11–12, 14–15; rapport with 12–14
pastor and scientist 153–4
pastors, mentors 102
Patton, M. Q. 46, 53, 56
perceptions 78
permeated learning (PL) theory 1, 4, 60, 104, 134, 142–3, 146–7, 156–9; African diaspora and desegregation 151–3; Legacy of Health (1888–1965) 149–51; literature review 155–6; pastor and scientist 153–4; recommendations 147–8; *vs.* transformational learning 144–5, *145*
Phi Beta Sigma 18, *18*, 50
poverty 37
prediabetes and diabetes 51
psychosocial interaction 138–9

qualitative research 43, 55–6
quantitative research 51

racial formation 19
Redwine, H. D. 21, 27
Rollins, K. 38
Ruder, K. 38

self-directed learning 9, 57, 137
self-efficacy 143
self-identity 38
siblings, mentors 93–4

sleepiness 71
Smith, A. B. 20, 29
social cognition 22
social constructivism 1–4, 9, 10, 17, 20, 22–3, 53, 138–9, 155; faith 112–16; fatalism 127–8; fear 120–2; fix 116–19; frustration 123–6; *see also* mentors
socialization 23
Soul Food 23
spirituality 1, 2, 10, 19, 25, 51, 143, 155, 156
spouse, mentors 92–3
Stewart, M. 41
Strauss, A. L 44–7, 79, 81, 84, 156
substantive living (SL) 104–7, *105*, **106**, 129–31, *130*, 133–4, 142, 143; and faith 107–16, 131–2; and fatalism 126–8, 133; and fear 119–22, 132; and fix 116–19, 132; and frustration 123–6, 133
Sunday school teacher 5, *5*
Swanson, R. A. 19
symbolic interactionism 45, 47, 53, 55–7, 76–8, 82, 86, 99, 105, 107

Taylor, L. M. 44, 45
theoretical framework 53–5
3D model: Afro-Theistic theory *130*; permeateted learning 143, 144, 149, 153–6
transformational learning, permeated learning theory *vs.* 144–5, *145*
trustworthiness 83–4
Two Feathers, J. G. 25, 35, 37, 38, 41, 42
type 2 diabetes mellitus (T2DM) 1, 6, 24, 35–7; Afro-Theistic faith and diabetes education 140; category 25; COGIC members 10; decision-making process 91; effects 68, 87; faith about 111, 116 (*see also* faith); fatalism (*see* fatalism); and fear 113, 114 (*see also* fear); fix (*see* fix); frustration (*see* frustration); on God 110; and obesity 63; symptom 71, 72; and youth 69, 73

Vella, J. 13, 83

Watson, J. 6
Weaver, E. H. 29–30
Weiler, D. M. 10, 138
Winant, H. 19

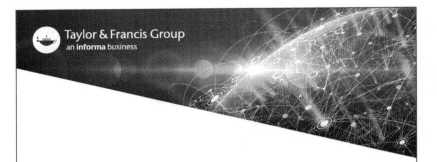

Printed in the United States
By Bookmasters